My Brilliant Body

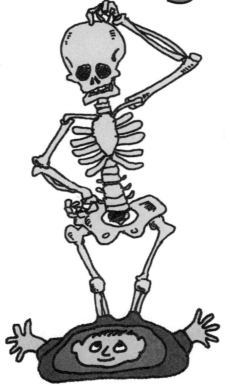

Written by Guy MacDonald
Illustrated by Paul Cemmick

BARRON'S

Written by Guy MacDonald
Illustrated by Paul Cemmick

First edition for the United States, its territories and possessions, Canada, and the Phillippines published in 2008 by Barron's Educational Series, Inc.

First published in Great Britain in 2008 by Buster Books, an imprint of Michael O'Mara Books Limited, 9 Lion Yard, Tremadoc Road, London SW4 7NQ

All inquiries should be addressed to:
Barron's Educational Series, Inc.
250 Wireless Blvd.
Hauppauge, NY 11788
www.barronseduc.com

Library of Congress Control Number: 2008925399

ISBN-13: 978-0-7641-6172-8
ISBN-10: 0-7641-6172-5

Printed in Canada
9 8 7 6 5 4 3 2 1

CONTENTS

CONTENTS

CONTENTS

CONTENTS

INTRODUCTION

Ever wonder what happens to your food after you eat it? Want to know the four signs that prove you are *actually* dead? Want to become a master farter? Or why you should keep your mouth closed at night?

The answers (including the gross stuff) to these and many more amazing questions about how we work are contained in *My Brilliant Body*. This book is filled with information from head to toe—and everything in between.

So, if you are ready to discover incredible things like the story of the man who ate a bicycle, or if you just want to know what to do if you have a nosebleed, then start reading. What follows is sure to surprise you and quite likely to disgust you!

HOW TO CHECK YOUR PULSE

Your pulse is the rhythm of your arteries filling with blood every time your heart beats. You can feel your pulse in the places on your body where the arteries are close to the skin, such as your wrist, neck, and temple. You can measure how fast your heart is beating by counting how many times your arteries fill with blood in one minute. Here is how to do it:

1. Make sure you are relaxed. Your heart beats faster when you are stressed, excited, or have been exercising.

2. Place the pads of two of your right-hand fingertips on the underside of your left wrist, in line with the bottom of your thumb.

3. Count the number of times you feel your artery beat in one minute. This is the same as your heartbeat.

4. Check the chart below to see if your pulse rate is healthy.

HEALTHY PULSE RATES

Ages one to ten.....................................60–140 beats per minute

Ages ten and up..................................60–100 beats per minute

Athletes...40–50 beats per minute

> There can be as many as 5.5 million red blood cells in one drop of blood.

> Starfish and sea urchins have no blood. Instead, they pump sea water around their bodies.

TASTE

You have around 10,000 receptors, known as taste buds, in your mouth. They are far too tiny to be seen. Taste buds are concentrated around the small pimples on the tongue, known as "papillae." The tongue can only detect four basic flavors—sweet, sour, salty, and bitter—although scientists have recently discovered what they think might be a fifth, savory flavor called "umami" or "yummy." Most flavors are a combination of smell and taste, which is why everything tastes the same when you have a cold and your nose is blocked.

TASTE BUDS

Different parts of your tongue detect different flavors.

Sour

Bitter

Salty

Sweet

The American Painted Lady butterfly has taste receptors on her feet. She walks on her food to taste it.

IN ONE HOUR

Tablespoons of saliva produced...3

Tablespoons of urine produced..5

Blood cells created and destroyed.......................8.3 million

Times you fart..1

Times you blink...600

Times you inhale...900

Times your heart beats..4,200

HUMAN WORMS

ROUNDWORMS
Look like pinkish-white earthworms. Can grow up to 12 inches (30 cm) long and be as thick as a pencil. Most commonly picked up on your hands from soil and transferred to your mouth.

WHIPWORMS
Curved like a whip, round in cross section and about 1–2 inches (2.5–5 cm) long. They get into your body through touching contaminated soil and unwashed vegetables.

PINWORMS
Small, threadlike, round, and white. They live inside your intestines and crawl out at night to lay their eggs between your butt cheeks.

HOOKWORMS
Get into the body through your feet, if you walk on ground contaminated by human waste. The larvae break through the skin into your bloodstream and work their way to the lungs, then the intestines.

TAPEWORMS
Flat and ribbony like tagliatelle pasta. Can grow up to 30 feet (9 m) long. Hide in uncooked pork, beef, or fish. Attach themselves to the wall of your intestine and absorb nutrients directly through their bodies.

BODY PARTS IN PROPORTION TO THEIR SENSITIVITY

The most sensitive areas of your body contain the most nerve endings in proportion to their size. These areas include your hands (particularly your fingertips), your head (particularly your lips and tongue), and your feet (particularly the soles and toes).

Your nose can detect up to 10,000 different smells. A smell can trigger your memory to recollect an event, along with the way you felt at the time.

THE FARTISTE

During the late nineteenth and early twentieth century, the Frenchman Joseph Pujol was famous for his ability to fart at will by drawing air into his anus. He put on a stage show, calling himself Le Pétomane, which is French for "The Fartiste." Dressed formally, he would open with a rumble of cannon-fire farting. Various routines followed, most spectacularly an imitation of the 1906 San Francisco earthquake. He could rectally project a jet of water a distance of 15 feet (4.5 m) and to close, he sang a rhyme about a farm, punctuated with farts that sounded like the different animal noises.

A CONVERSATION BETWEEN FARTERS

"He who smelled it dealt it."

"He who denied it supplied it."

"Whoever said the rhyme did the crime."

"The smeller's the feller!"

"He who detected it ejected it!"

"Let's agree it was me."

DREAMS

Dreaming is believed to be a way of managing your memories, feelings, and thoughts. It helps you to file away new experiences and recall old ones.

You have five or six dreams a night and, on average, a dream lasts 20 minutes.

During your lifetime you will spend about 20 years sleeping. During the 20 years you spend sleeping, you will watch around 150,000 dreams.

You are more likely to have nightmares toward morning.

THE YAWN IDENTITY

Your mouth stretches as if you want to eat your own head. Air rushes into your lungs and out again. Your eyes fill. It lasts about five seconds. But what is a yawn? Strangely, the yawn remains one of the great unsolved mysteries. It is thought to be due to your body wanting oxygen. You yawn because you are tired, bored, nervous, or about to vomit or faint. You yawn when you see someone else yawning. Reading about yawning can make you want to yawn. You are probably thinking about yawning now. Thinking about yawning makes you want to yawn. You want to yawn. You'd love to yawn. You are going to yawn.

The scientific word for yawning is "pandiculation."

REASONS TO CLOSE YOUR MOUTH AT NIGHT

Cockroaches · Mosquitoes · Houseflies · Earwigs
Lice · Weevils · Beetles · Fleas · Ants · Spiders

WHAT'S GROWING ON THE FOOT FARM?

Tight shoes and sweaty trainers are growbags
for foot life...

VERRUCAS (WARTS)
Caused by a virus that
gets into the body
through cracks in the
soles of your feet.
Covered with black dots,
which are blood vessels
that feed it.

ATHLETE'S FOOT
Itchy rash caused
by fungus that nibbles
away at the dead skin
between your toes.

CORNS AND CALLUSES
Crusty bits of skin
that form on your
feet because of constant
pressure from shoes.

INGROWN TOENAILS
Your big toenail grows into
your skin like a splinter. If
it is not removed,
infection follows.

BUNIONS
A bump that sprouts on
the side of your big toe if
it shifts to the side. It can
be corrected with surgery.

BLISTERS
Try not to pop them!
The watery stuff is fluid
released from tiny blood
vessels when the skin is
under attack from rubbing
or burning. It protects
the damaged skin while
repairs go on underneath.

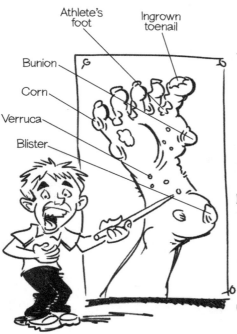

Athlete's foot

Ingrown toenail

Bunion

Corn

Verruca

Blister

WHAT'S IN THE FIRST-AID BOX?

Cotton ball...Cleaning wounds

Tweezers..Removing splinters

Scissors..Cutting bandages

Dressings and bandages....................................Covering wounds

Safety pins...Holding dressings in place

An eye bath................................Rinsing chemicals out of eyes

Antiseptic cream..........Protects minor cuts against infection

Elastic bandage...Supporting sprains

Adhesive dressings....................Covering cuts while they heal

WHAT TO DO IF SOMEONE FAINTS

1. Lie the person down, turn their head to the side, and raise and support their legs.

2. Make sure there is plenty of fresh air.

3. Reassure them that they are OK and gradually help them to sit up.

WHAT TO DO IF SOMEONE IS CHOKING

1. Stand behind the person, make a fist and place it just below their breastbone.

2. Then grasp your fist with your other hand and press into the chest up to five times with a sharp inward and upward thrust, once every three seconds.

3. Repeat this procedure until the person coughs up the obstruction in their throat. This is known as the Heimlich maneuver.

HOW TO SHRINK A HEAD

The Jivaro tribe of Ecuador, South America, would shrink the severed heads of their enemies after battle. Here's how to do it.

1. Open the skin at the back of the head and remove the skull.

2. Sew up the eyes and lips.

3. Cook the head in special herbs and water for about two hours.

4. Fill the head with hot sand or pebbles.

5. Hang the head over a smoldering fire.

6. Over several days the head will shrink to the size of a man's fist, while retaining the recognizable features of the slain warrior.

STRANGE APPETITES

Some people get cravings to eat unexpected things. Young children and pregnant women are the worst offenders. The cravings can be very peculiar.

Acuphagia	Sharp objects
Coniophagia	Dust
Coprophagia	Poo
Geomelophagia	Raw potatoes
Geophagia	Soil, coal, chalk
Lithophagia	Stones
Mucophagia	Boogers
Pagophagia	Ice
Trichophagia	Hair
Xylophagia	Wood

THE MAN WHO ATE A BICYCLE

Since 1959, Frenchman Michel Lotito, who calls himself Monsieur Mangetout, has been eating metal and glass objects. It is said that his stomach and intestinal walls are twice the normal thickness, and his digestive acids are unusually potent. He cuts the objects into tiny pieces and consumes roughly 2 pounds of material per day. It can take him months or even years to consume large objects. Here are some of the things he has eaten:

18 bicycles • 7 TV sets

2 beds • 1 pair of skis

15 supermarket shopping carts

1 Cessna light aircraft.

Dung beetles feed on animal droppings. Some dung beetles shape a lump of poo into a ball, roll it into their burrow, then lay their eggs in it.

THE INCREDIBLE JOURNEY OF A SANDWICH

MOUTH: your teeth grind the sandwich and your salivary glands produce a fountain of spit. Chemicals in the spit start to turn the bread into sugars. Your tongue pushes the food to the back of your throat and you swallow.

THROAT: muscle action pushes the wet lump of food down your "esophagus" to your stomach.

STOMACH: the pulped food is churned over and over with acids and chemicals that help break it down. A valve at the bottom of your stomach releases the semidigested food into the small intestine.

SMALL INTESTINE: chemicals from your liver and pancreas continue to break the food down into tiny particles. Small sponge-like fingers called "villi" absorb the nutrients into your bloodstream. Any leftover food moves into your large intestine.

LARGE INTESTINE: the leftover mush is broken down by bacteria into waste (called feces). It gets harder and drier as water is sucked out of it and absorbed into your body.

RECTUM: The feces gather at the end of the large intestine and wait there to be pooped out.

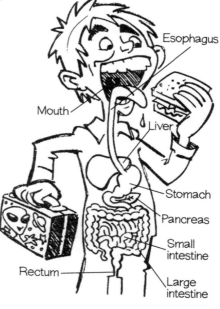

Esophagus

Mouth

Liver

Stomach

Pancreas

Small intestine

Rectum

Large intestine

DIGESTION

During your lifetime you will digest around
20 tons (20,000 kg) of food.

The job of the digestive system is to break down
the foods you eat into molecules that your body
can use for energy, growth, and repair.

The digestive system is also known as the
"alimentary canal." It runs from your mouth to your
anus via your esophagus, stomach, and intestines.

Your stomach is J-shaped. When it is empty, it
can be as small as a fist. After a meal it can
stretch to be almost as big as a football.

The muscle action that pushes food through
your alimentary canal is called "peristalsis." This
is the same muscle action that an earthworm
uses to wriggle.

The digestive fluid that breaks down proteins in
the stomach contains hydrochloric acid. Your
stomach wall is also partly made from proteins,
but a coating of protective mucus stops it
from digesting itself.

THE TIME FOOD SPENDS IN THE DIGESTIVE SYSTEM

Mouth	3-30 seconds
Esophagus	4-8 seconds
Stomach	2-4 hours
Small intestine	3-5 hours
Large intestine	10 hours to several days
Rectum	1-20 minutes

SPACE SICKNESS

MOTION SICKNESS
During weightlessness, your feet and ankles no longer signal the direction of down, so you can feel as if you are the wrong way up.

MUSCLE WASTAGE
On Earth, bones and muscles are always working against gravity. In space, muscles don't have to work as hard so they start to waste away.

FEELING FLUISH
On Earth, gravity normally concentrates fluid in your legs and stomach. In space, fluid sits more in your chest and head, causing your neck veins to bulge, your face to go puffy, and your nose to feel blocked.

SMALL HEART
The heart doesn't have to pump as hard in zero gravity and reduces its size by a third.

CRUMBLY BONES
On Earth, your body knows which parts of the skeleton need to be especially strong. Being in zero gravity confuses this. After a very long voyage in space, it's thought that your skeleton would be unable to support the weight of your body when you returned to Earth.

DECREASED IMMUNITY
The number of white blood cells in the body mysteriously decreases during a space voyage. White blood cells fight infection, so space travelers are particularly vulnerable to illness.

Between 1984 and 1990, the deadly E. coli bacteria survived on board a special satellite in orbit around the Earth for six years.

STRETCHY SKIN

British man Gary Turner has a rare skin disorder that makes his skin incredibly stretchy. He can stretch the skin on his stomach to a length of about 6 inches (16 cm). By pulling the skin of his neck up and the skin of his forehead down, he can completely cover his whole face. In 2004, he clipped 159 ordinary wooden clothespins to his face, earning himself a world record.

HORRIBLE HAIR

It is normal to lose up to 100 hairs per day.

Microscopic hairs at the back of your nose sweep mucus toward your throat.

Pubic hair is short and curly with a coarse texture.

Hair appears to continue growing for several days after death as the tissues around the hair follicles dehydrate and the skin recedes.

Hair shafts can store poisons for years after death.

A lock of a deceased loved one's hair is sometimes kept as a *memento mori* (reminder of death).

SKIN

The skin is the largest organ in the body.

If it were laid out flat, a fully-grown man's skin would cover approximately 20 square feet (6 square meters).

Moles are brown blobs of a substance called "melanin." Melanin is the skin's sun-defense system. It darkens to protect the skin against sunburn. Freckles are also blobs of melanin that darken in the sun.

During your lifetime your body will shed around 44 pounds (20 kg) of waste skin.

Around half of all house dust is made up of human skin.

Belly-button fluff is made from clothing fibers that stick to the sweat that your body produces. The fibers stay tucked inside your belly button even after the sweat has dried.

> The skin on a badger's bottom is so baggy that if it is grabbed from behind by a fox the badger is able to twist around and bite back.

HOW TO BE A MASTER FARTER

1. Lie on the floor on your belly with your head to one side on a pillow.

2. Bring your bottom into the air and your knees up as close to your head as possible. Relax.

3. When you feel the strange sensation of air entering your colon, you are in business. Gently push the air out of your anus. More air will enter.

4. Soon you will be inhaling and exhaling through your anus. With practice, this can also be accomplished sitting down.

SCALPING

Native Americans used to cut the skin off the heads of their enemies, hair and all. They would pin their enemy to the ground with a knee in their back, then pull back the head by the hair. Using a sharp scalping knife they would then cut a circle of skin from the head. The operation was not fatal, but more often than not the enemy was already dying of other wounds. The scalp was then dried out and the hair groomed and it was kept as a trophy of war.

The Ancient Greeks used to make themselves cloaks by sewing together the scalps of their fallen enemies.

Human hair grows about 0.02 in. (0.5 mm) per day. Hot weather makes it grow faster. The hair on your head can grow up to 6 in. (15 cm) per year. Waist-length hair is 31-35 in. (80-90 cm) long and will have taken about 6 years to grow.

THE FOUR SIGNS YOU'RE DEFINITELY DEAD

LIVOR MORTIS

Occurs when the heart stops pumping blood around the body, and the heavy red blood cells sink down into the legs. This causes a purplish discoloration of the skin. It starts between 20 minutes and 3 hours after death.

ALGOR MORTIS

The reduction in body temperature that follows death. There is generally a steady drop down to room temperature.

RIGOR MORTIS

Caused by a chemical change in the muscles. The limbs become stiff and impossible to move. It usually sets in about 3 to 4 hours after death, and eventually relaxes after about 36 hours.

DECOMPOSITION

Begins at the moment of death, when internal chemicals and bacteria begin to break down the body's tissues. These processes release gases that swell the body and produce a horrible odor. An adult body buried in ordinary soil without a coffin will take 10 to 12 years to become a skeleton.

WHAT ARE YOU MADE OF?

Percentage of Human Body.................Where Else It Is Found

Oxygen 65%...The ozone layer

Carbon 18.5%...Diamonds

Hydrogen 9.5%...Water

Nitrogen 3.3%...Fertilizer

Calcium 1.5%...Chalk

Phosphorus 1%...Matches

Potassium 0.4%...Fireworks

Sulphur 0.3%..Gunpowder

Chlorine 0.2%..Bleach

Sodium 0.2%..Salt

Magnesium 0.1%...Indigestion medicines

Iron 0.004%...Bridges

Iodine 0.00004%..Antiseptics

Silicon (trace)..................................Computer circuit boards

Fluorine (trace)...................................Non-stick frying pans

Copper (trace)..Coins

Manganese (trace)...Batteries

Zinc (trace)..Motorway crash barriers

Selenium (trace)...............................Anti-dandruff shampoo

Cobalt (trace)......................................Blue glass and ceramics

Molybdenum (trace)...................................Flame retardant

Boron (trace)..Heat-proof glass

MIND OVER MATTER

This is the belief that the mind is more powerful
than the body. It allows people to perform
incredible feats such as:

Walking over hot coals with bare feet

Lying on a bed of nails

Undergoing operations without anesthetic

Breaking wooden planks with a kung-fu chop

Lifting a car to free an accident victim

> Every day your mouth makes
> enough spit to fill a lunch box.

THE UNBENDABLE ARM

Is your mind stronger than your body? Can you make
your arm unbendable?

1. Hold your arm out to one side, slightly bent at the
   elbow, with your thumb facing upward.

2. Relax as much as you can without your arm dropping.

3. Now look down the length of your arm.

4. Try to imagine that it extends in a straight line for
   miles and miles. Imagine you are poking someone in
   the ribs in the next street.

5. Holding on to this relaxed, stretched feeling, ask a
   friend to try to bend your arm.

6. If your mind is stronger than your body your friend
   won't be able to bend your arm however physically
   strong he or she may be.

BAD BREATH

Stale morning breath is the smell of bacteria that have been partying in your mouth overnight. The bacteria can get away with this because, when you sleep, the production of saliva in your mouth slows down, and saliva contains chemicals that would normally combat bacteria.

SO IT HAS A NAME

LUNULA
The white half-moon
shapes on your nails.

FRENULUM
Strip of tissue connecting
your tongue to the
bottom of your mouth.

PHILTRUM
The skin between the
nose and the top lip.

SCLERA
The white of the eye.

FOSSETTE
Dimple on chin.

HEAD LICE

Head lice are tiny six-legged insects that can be up to one-tenth of an inch (3 mm) long.

They grip onto hairs with their pincers and feed on blood sucked from the head.

They can change color to look darker in dark hair.

They eat for 45 seconds every 4 to 6 hours.

Female lice lay their eggs at the base of the hairs, and each egg becomes firmly attached to a hair shaft.

The eggs are called nits. It is almost impossible to comb them out.

In their 30-day life span, each female louse lays 200-300 eggs. The eggs take ten days to hatch.

Head lice like clean hair.

Dandruff is not caused by having a dry scalp. It occurs when your body's immune system makes your skin flake in response to a fungus called malassezia.

WOUNDS

INCISION: a clean cut from a sharp edge that bleeds a lot.

LACERATION: a rough tear from a ripping or crushing force that bruises and bleeds.

GRAZE: a scrape along the top layer of the skin.

"BLACK AND BLUE": broken blood vessels under the skin caused by a heavy blow. The skin is not broken.

PUNCTURE: a small but deep stab wound from a sharp object.

GUNSHOT: a deep internal injury from a bullet.

IN A DOCTOR'S BAG

Stethoscope...To listen to heart and lungs

Tongue depressor..............To hold down tongue to see tonsils

Digital thermometer......................................To take temperature

Tuning fork...To check for hearing loss

Glucometer.....................................To measure blood-sugar level

Sphygmomanometer........................To measure blood pressure

Otoscope.....To see into ear with a light and magnifying lens

Peak flow meter..........................To measure ability to breathe

Ophthalmoscope................To see into the back of the eyes

Rubber hammer............................To tap knee and test reflexes

TEST YOUR REFLEXES

1. Rest one leg loosely over the other.
2. Lightly tap the top leg just below its kneecap.
3. The leg jerks forward.
4. The leg falls back.

At least it should...

PUBERTY

BOYS	GIRLS
Voice breaks and then deepens.	Voice deepens a little.
Hair appears on the face and body.	Hair appears on the body.
Muscles grow.	Fatty tissue forms on the breasts, hips, and thighs.
Shoulders broaden.	Breasts develop.
Sperm is produced in the testes.	Hips and pelvis widen.
	Menstrual cycle begins.

BODY ODOR

Puberty activates sweat glands known as "apocrine" glands in the armpits and groin. At moments of stress, high emotion, exercise, or sexual excitement, they secrete an odorless milky substance, which only starts to stink when bacteria get hold of it.

WHAT TO DO IF YOU HAVE A NOSEBLEED

1. Clear out all the blood by having a good snort, cough, and sniff.

2. Breathe through your mouth and pinch your nose shut.

3. Keep holding it shut for ten minutes. DO NOT cough, spit, or peek to see if bleeding has stopped.

4. Use a clean tissue to mop up the blood.

5. Don't pick the scab or it will start again.

ZITS

Zits form in hair follicles. Hair follicles contain "sebaceous" glands to help keep the skin supple. Hormones during puberty can make these glands produce excess oil and wax, known as sebum. If the duct leading from the gland to the skin's surface becomes blocked with dead cells or hardened sebum, you are in trouble. At its mildest, a tiny bump or blackhead will form. If the surrounding skin becomes infected, a red, pus-filled spot will appear. Pus is formed from white blood cells sent to kill the bacteria.

A male emperor moth can smell the odor of a female moth 3 miles (5 km) away.

SMELL

Smells are tiny particles, too small to be seen. As you inhale, you draw them into your nose. There, they are picked up by millions of nerve endings, which relay signals to the brain. Your brain tells you what is being smelled.

REAL POISONS

Cyanide • Opium • Sulphur • Mercury • Arsenic • Lead
Laurel berries • Hellebore • Fool's Parsley

MYTHICAL POISONS

Swamp frogs • Chicks stung to death by hornets
Crocodiles bitten to death by snakes • Salamanders
Mice stung to death by scorpions • Eel brains
Black crows drowned in brine • Leopard's gall bladder
Cats' brains • Menstrual blood

POISONING TRICKS

In Ancient Rome, poisoners wore rings with hinged lids called "poison rings." The murderer would wait until the victim wasn't looking, then unfasten the lid and tip the poison into the victim's wine.

It is said that the Roman Emperor Augustus died after eating a fig from his garden. Every single one had been injected with a deadly poison.

In the Middle Ages, European ladies used to carry bags of perfumed flowers called nosegays, which they could smell if there was a disgusting odor in the air. It was easy for poisoners to add a substance that could kill with one sniff.

Poison knives are ingenious inventions that can instantly kill a victim. When the slightest pressure is placed on the cutting edge of the blade, three tiny, poison-tipped needles are driven into the victim's hand.

WAYS TO PRESERVE A BODY

PLASTIC: A technique called "plastination" has been developed to permanently preserve human corpses. The bodies are saturated in resins in a vacuum and can be positioned in any pose.

MUMMIFICATION: In Ancient Egypt, wealthy or powerful people sometimes had their internal organs removed after death. The organs were individually embalmed using a substance called natron, which dried them out and discouraged bacteria. The body was then embalmed in the same way, stuffed to give it shape, stitched back up and wrapped in bandages.

BOG: Usually when we die, bacteria and other germs eat away at our skin and muscles leaving only our bones behind which eventually dissolve too. Under some natural conditions, such as those found in peat bogs, the bacteria necessary for decomposition do not grow, and bodies are found hundreds or even thousands of years after death.

ICE: Ice also prevents bacteria from decomposing the body. The bodies of three Austrian soldiers from the First World War were recently found in the ice over 11,000 feet (3,300 m) high on the San Matteo mountain in Italy. It is thought the men were killed by a grenade during a battle in 1918.

THE MAN WITH A LID ON HIS STOMACH

On June 6, 1822, an 18-year-old Canadian soldier was accidentally shot in the stomach at close range. His breakfast poured out of a hole the size of a large coin. The army surgeon William Beaumont saved the soldier's life, but the hole in his stomach wouldn't heal properly. A flap grew over it that could be opened and shut by hand. Beaumont realized that this provided a rare chance to study human digestion. He put foods into the soldier's stomach on a string, and then removed them to see what had been digested, and how fast.

Why fart and waste it when you can burp and taste it?

THE STOOL FORM SCALE

"The Stool Form Scale" was developed at the University of Bristol, England. It is a guide to the seven most common types of stool. (A stool is a piece of feces. Feces is the scientific word for poo.)

Type one..........Separate hard lumps, like nuts (hard to pass)

Type two...Sausage-shaped, but lumpy

Type three.....Like a sausage, but with cracks on its surface

Type four...............Like a sausage or snake, smooth and soft

Type five.........Soft blobs with smooth edges (passed easily)

Type six........Fluffy pieces with ragged edges, a mushy stool

Type seven....................Watery, no solid pieces, entirely liquid

As a rough guide, if you are constipated (finding it difficult to squeeze out a poo) you will struggle and perhaps produce a type one or two. If you have diarrhea, expect frequent eruptions of type six or seven. A healthy bowel releases a type three or four every day or so.

GARDEZ L'EAU!

In the Middle Ages there were no flushing toilets. Human waste went into a pot, and when the pot was full, its contents were simply thrown out of the window. Before it was emptied, passersby were warned to get out of the way quickly by the cry, "Gardez l'eau," which is French for "Mind the water." At that point, only very stupid people looked up.

Moreover, in the Middle Ages, aristocratic women used goose feathers for toilet paper.

THE SMELLY-BREATH DETECTOR

The "Fresh Kiss" is a hand-held gadget sold in Japan. The user breathes into one end and the gadget then displays a reading from a scale ranging from "undetectable" to "very smelly."

THE HEART

Your heart is located almost in the center of your chest, between your lungs. It is not far over on your left side as many people think.

Your heart is a pump with four chambers. It pumps oxygen-poor blood from your body to your lungs to be loaded with oxygen, and oxygen-rich blood from your lungs around your body.

To make sure that your blood only flows in one direction through your heart, valves separate the four chambers and stop the blood from flowing backward. The boom-boom noise that your heart makes is the sound of these valves banging shut.

Electrical impulses from cells in your heart trigger your heartbeat. If these cells stop working, a doctor can insert a small battery that does the same job.

The human heart beats around 100,000 times per day, and 2.5 billion times in an average lifetime.

Blood takes approximately 60 seconds to go around the entire body.

BLOOD VESSELS

ARTERIES: take oxygen-rich blood away from the heart to the body.

VEINS: take oxygen-poor blood from the body to the heart.

CAPILLARIES: are the smallest blood vessels in the human body. They connect arteries to body tissue and body tissue to veins. They have very thin walls through which some molecules can pass. This allows oxygen and water to pass from the blood into the body's tissues, and waste products to pass back into the blood to be taken away and disposed of by organs such as the lungs and kidneys.

THE THREE TYPES OF BLEEDING

ARTERIAL BLEEDING

Arteries contain bright red, oxygen-rich blood. Blood in the arteries is under a lot of pressure because it has recently been pumped from the heart. A severed main artery will jet blood several feet high in time with the heartbeat.

VENOUS BLEEDING

Veins contain dark red, oxygen-poor blood. Blood in the veins is under less pressure than blood in the arteries because it has not been pumped straight from the heart, but has come through the capillaries from body tissues. Nevertheless, blood will gush from a severed vein.

CAPILLARY BLEEDING

This type of bleeding is usually the result of a scrape, although, when capillaries under the skin rupture and bleed into the tissues, you get a bruise. Not much blood is lost.

HUMAN BABY SKILLS

3-8 weeks...................Smiles in response to faces and noises

2-4 months.....................Raises shoulders when lying on belly

5-6 months....................................Starts making babbling noises

4-7 months....................................Rolls over from front to back

8-12 months..Crawls at speed

10-12 months.............................Stands when holding something

11-13 months..Stands unsupported

12-16 months...Walks without help

16-18 months...Follows simple instructions

BEASTLY BABIES

CUCKOOS

The cuckoo lays its eggs in another bird's nest to save it from having to rear its own young.

SHARKS

Some unborn sharks eat each other inside their mother. As soon as the shark pups have developed functional mouths and stomachs, the strongest pup eats the remaining unfertilized eggs. When there are no more eggs left, it starts to eat its brothers and sisters. In the end, only one strong pup survives.

SEA HORSES

Female sea horses lay their eggs in a male's pouch. The male then carries the unborn sea horses until they are ready to emerge two to six weeks later.

DIGGER WASPS

These wasps build a nest in the ground and stock it with captured insects before laying their eggs. The prey are kept alive, paralyzed with wasp toxins. When the wasp larvae hatch, they feed on the paralyzed insects before leaving the nest.

STRONGMEN

Australian David Huxley pulled a Boeing 747-400 weighing 190 tons (190,000 kg) for a distance of a little more than half a mile (91 m) in just 1 minute.

Zafar Gill from Pakistan lifted 114 pounds (51.7 kg) of gym weights using only his ear.

England's John Evans balanced a 351.9 pound (159.6 kg) Mini Cooper car on his head for 33 seconds.

Tom Leppard of Scotland has had his whole body tattooed with a leopard-skin design.

BODY MASS INDEX

Your Body Mass Index (BMI) is a measure used to tell whether you are a healthy weight. To work it out, divide your weight in pounds by your height in inches squared, and then multiply by 703. Here is the equation:

BMI = mass in pounds / (height in inches x height in inches x 703)

BMI below 18.5 = Underweight

BMI 18.5-24.9 = Average

BMI 25-29.9 = Overweight

BMI 30 and above = Obese.

LEECHES

Leeches are slug-like animals that live on land, in the sea, and in fresh water. Some types of leech feed on the blood of other animals, including humans. These leeches grip onto the skin with suckers and can drink up to three times their body weight in blood. Until the nineteenth century, doctors used leeches to treat many illnesses. The cure for everything from headaches to eczema was to let a hungry leech gorge on the patient's blood. Modern medicine has rediscovered the wonders of leeches in certain cases. When severed body parts are reattached, for example, leeches can be used to absorb excess blood and to keep the blood flowing.

BLOODY LEECH FACTS

There are more than 650 known species of leeches.

The medical leech has 300 teeth and 32 brains.

The bite of a leech is painless because it injects its own anesthetic.

After a leech drops off, the wound it leaves will bleed for around ten hours.

Leeches can go several months between feeds.

The largest leech ever measured 18 inches (46 cm).

THE VOMIT COMET

"The Vomit Comet" was the nickname of the aircraft used by NASA between 1973 and 1995 to train astronauts at zero gravity. By diving from a great height in an arc, the plane gave astronauts about 25 seconds of weightlessness. During those 25 seconds, however, many of the astronauts decorated the cabin walls with their lunch.

TEN PHRASES FOR VOMITING

Blowing chunks • Shout at your shoes

Technicolor yawn • Facial diarrhea • Feed the floor

Liquidate your assets • Decorate the pavement

Deliver a street pizza

The record holder for projectile vomiting spewed his stomach contents a distance of 26 feet (8 m).

WAYS TO STOP YOURSELF FROM VOMITING

Sip ginger ale • Suck a mint

Eat plain crackers • Look at the horizon

Press on the inside of your wrist

Every time you smell a fart, you are inhaling particles from the farter's bottom.

SNEEZES

A sneeze is your nose's way of getting rid of something super-quickly.

Germs from a sneeze can hang around in the air for an hour.

If you sneeze with your eyes open, your eyeballs do not pop out.

One sneeze can contain 6 million viruses.

The world's sneezing record is held by a 12-year-old British girl who sneezed for two and a half years, from 1981 to 1983. She sneezed approximately one million times a year.

STEROIDS

Steroids are chemicals that occur naturally in the body and can also be made in a laboratory. They include the male sex hormone testosterone and the female sex hormone estrogen. Anabolic steroids are made from testosterone and were originally designed to help dangerously thin patients put on weight. Some body builders and athletes take anabolic steroids to help build up their muscles. Not only is this cheating, it is also dangerous and can trigger heart attacks and kidney failure early in life.

WHAT'S IN BLOOD?

Red blood cells...Carry oxygen

White blood cells..Fight infection

Platelets....................................Form clots to help stop bleeding

Plasma...................Carries nutrients, enzymes, and hormones

DON'T BE A SQUIRT

On September 1, 2004, Ilker Yilmaz of Turkey squirted milk from her eye a distance of 9 ft. 1 in. (2.795 m).

WHERE IS IT MADE?

Urine is made in your kidneys.

Poo is made in your intestines.

Sweat is made in glands in your skin.

Blood is made in your bone marrow.

TEST YOUR EYES

A

36

D F

24

H Z P

18

T X U D

12

Z A D N H

9

P N T U H X

6

U A Z N F D T

5

N P H T A F X U

4

X D F H P T Z A N

3

Stand about 7 feet (2.25 m) from the chart. If you can read down to the seventh line your vision is normal. If you can read all the way to the bottom line your vision is better than average. (If you can't read the top line you should make an appointment with an optician right away!)

CPR

CPR is a very valuable lifesaving technique. What follows are general instructions; it is smart to take a course to become fully trained. You could save a life. NOTE: CPR for infants and children is performed differently. If a person seems to be unconscious, make sure that someone calls the emergency services and check for signs of life. Watch the chest to see if it is rising and falling and listen for breathing sounds. Try putting your face close to his or her mouth to determine if you can feel the breath on your cheek. If you can't see any signs of breathing, check the pulse to find out if the heart is beating. Do this by pressing the pads of your index and middle fingers onto the underside of their wrist, just below the base of their thumb. If there is no pulse you need to keep the person alive artificially using a technique called "cardio-pulmonary resuscitation" (CPR). There are two parts to this technique: chest compressions, which keep the blood circulating around the body, and mouth-to-mouth ventilation, which fills the lungs with air.

HOW TO GIVE CHEST COMPRESSIONS

1. Find where the bottom of the person's breastbone meets his or her ribs, and place the heel of your hand two finger widths above this point.
2. Place the heel of one hand on top of your other hand, and interlock your fingers.
3. Leaning well over the person, with your arms straight, press vertically down and depress the casualty's breastbone about 1-1/2 to 2 inches (approx. 4.5 cm). Release the pressure without removing your hands.
4. Compress the chest 30 times in fairly quick succession, then give two breaths of artificial ventilation. Continue the cycle of 30 chest compressions, followed by two breaths of mouth-to-mouth, until help arrives.

HOW TO GIVE MOUTH-TO-MOUTH

1. Look into the person's mouth and remove any blockage in the airway.

2. Open the person's airway by tilting back the head and gently lifting the chin with your fingers.

3. Keep the head tilted back and pinch the nostrils shut. Now take a deep breath and place your lips around the mouth, taking care to make a seal.

4. Blow evenly into the mouth for about one second until the chest rises as far as it will go.

5. Remove your lips and let the chest deflate. Repeat once before checking the pulse and breathing.

6. If there is a pulse but still no sign of breathing, continue breathing for the person until help arrives.

7. If there is no pulse or breathing, keep repeating the cycle, including chest compressions, until help arrives.

WARNING
Never practice this on a friend—take a course to be a truly proficient lifesaver

---

THE SCIENCE OF GROSS

Bromhidrosis..Body odor

Erophagia...Swallowing air then belching

Halitosis..Smelly breath

Cerumen..Ear wax

Tinea pedis..Athlete's foot

Vibrissae...Nose hair

Rhinotillexomania..Nose picking

Mucophagy...Eating boogers

MAGGOTS

It was once thought that maggots grew from rotting meat. An Italian physician called Francesco Redi devised an experiment to show that this couldn't be true. He placed a piece of meat in each of three flasks. He left one of the flasks open, another one tightly sealed, and the last one covered with gauze. After a few days, the meat in the open flask was crawling with maggots, and the gauze-covered flask had maggots on the surface of the gauze. The tightly sealed flask, however, was completely free of maggots inside and out. From this he concluded that it was the flies that produced the maggots, not the rotting meat.

Some types of maggot are used to clear dead tissue out of wounds that won't heal. They eat only dead flesh, leaving the living tissue unaffected. It is important not to use the wrong sort of maggot, however, as some will eat live flesh.

CHILDHOOD DISEASES

CHICKEN POX
Cause: virus
Symptoms: high temperature, red and itchy spots or blisters over the entire body.
Contagious: two to three days before the symptoms occur until the blisters crust over.

MEASLES
Cause: virus
Symptoms: high temperature, runny nose, cough, sore and reddened eyes. The rash usually starts on the face and spreads down the body, and lasts three or more days.
Contagious: four days before symptoms appear to five days after the rash starts.

WHOOPING COUGH
Cause: bacteria
Symptoms: long coughing fits followed by wheezy breathing and sometimes vomiting. Worse at night.
Contagious: from the first sneezes until the patient is cured.

SCARLET FEVER
Cause: bacteria
Symptoms: high temperature, sore throat and a coarse, pink tongue known as "strawberry tongue."
Contagious: two to four days before symptoms appear, but after five days of antibiotics the risk is almost gone.

RUBELLA (GERMAN MEASLES)
Cause: virus
Symptoms: a mild temperature, aching body and head, and often a rash.
Contagious: from a week before to five days after symptoms appear.

MUMPS
Cause: virus
Symptoms: swollen glands in jaw, cheeks, and neck, accompanied by high temperature and headache.
Contagious: from about a week before symptoms appear to a week afterward.

URINE

You produce about 2.6 pints (1.5 liters) of urine every day.

Urine is stored in the bladder, and as the bladder fills up it stretches like a balloon. When this happens, nerve messages are sent from the wall of the bladder to the brain, to let you know that it needs emptying.

When you pee, several different muscles are used. First your stomach muscles press on your bladder. Then your diaphragm descends, making you hold your breath. Finally your pelvic floor muscles relax and urine passes out of your body through a tube called the urethra.

The technical term for wetting the bed is "nocturnal enuresis."

KIDNEYS

Your kidneys remove all the unwanted water, salt, and chemicals from your blood so that they can be expelled from the body as urine. Your kidneys filter about 317 pints (180 liters) of blood every day.

Diabetes mellitus is a disease caused by lack of a hormone called "insulin." The body needs insulin to control the level of sugar in the blood. The disease can cause problems with the kidneys, eyesight, and blood flow, and can even lead to coma or death. Diabetes mellitus means "passing through sweetly," and people with untreated diabetes have sugary pee and breath that smells of pear drops. Medieval doctors used to taste their patients' pee to check for the illness.

BIG MEDICAL BREAKTHROUGHS

Circulation of the blood............William Harvey, 1628, England

Vaccination...................................Edward Jenner, 1796, England

Antiseptic...Joseph Lister, 1867, Scotland

X-ray.........................Wilhelm Conrad Röntgen, 1895, Germany

Antibiotics...............................Alexander Fleming, 1928, England

Structure of DNA...................Crick and Watson, 1953, England

We use our tongues to make different sounds when we speak. For example, to make a "t" sound you have to put the tip of your tongue on the roof of your mouth. To make a "th" sound, your tongue has to be between your teeth.

TONGUES

The tongue is one of the strongest muscles in the human body.

White spots on the tongue or a yellow tongue can be an indication of illness.

Can you roll your tongue into a hollow tube? The ability to roll your tongue is genetic, like the color of your eyes. You can either do it, or you can't.

A crocodile cannot stick its tongue out.

A chameleon's tongue can be more than one and a half times the length of its body.

Some animals have blue tongues, including the Blue-tongued lizard and the Chow Chow dog.

A blue whale's tongue is about the size and weight of a full-grown African elephant.

A snore can reach a volume of 90 decibels. That's almost as loud as a pneumatic drill.

CANNIBALISM

Cannibalism is the practice of eating other members of the same species.

During the nineteenth century, the Fijian chief Ratu Udre Udre ate between 872 and 999 people. He liked to eat every part of his victim in one sitting.

The Korowai tribe of Papua is one of the last surviving tribes in the world said to practice cannibalism.

The habit of biting your nails or pieces of skin from your fingers is sometimes identified as cannibalism.

Some mothers eat the placenta (the organ that connects the unborn baby's blood supply to the mother's) once their child is born.

Rabbits, mice, rats, and hamsters will eat their young if predators repeatedly threaten their nest.

Some octopuses, toads, salamanders, crocodiles, fish, and spiders prey on smaller and weaker animals of their own species.

Female black widow spiders and praying mantises sometimes eat the male after mating.

THE LANGUAGE OF DISEASE

ANTIBODIES
Proteins produced by the immune system that help to fight infections.

IMMUNITY
The ability to resist a particular infection or toxin by the action of specific antibodies or white blood cells.

INCUBATION
The development of an infection from when it first enters the body to the first signs of disease.

VACCINATION
A weakened or dead form of a disease introduced to the body to encourage the production of antibodies against it.

ENDEMIC
The constant presence of a disease in a community or geographical area.

EPIDEMIC
A sudden and widespread outbreak of a disease in a certain region.

PANDEMIC
An epidemic that affects a wide geographical area.

CARRIER
A person who does not show any symptoms of a disease, but who carries it and can pass it on to others.

THE TIMELINE OF AN UNBORN HUMAN

Conception.......................A sperm fertilizes the mother's egg

1 week...................Fertilized egg settles in the mother's womb

4 weeks..................Spine and nervous system begin to form

8 weeks........................Ears, eyes, and limbs start to develop

10 weeks...Fetus is recognizably human

12 weeks...........................Nails, eyebrows, and eyelashes form

16 weeks.............Limbs move freely, fetus is about 6 inches (15 cm) long

28 weeks...........................A layer of fat forms under the skin

30 weeks.......................................Fetus can tell light from dark

34 weeks...........................Baby is head-down, ready for birth

38 weeks...........................Baby's lungs are fully formed

40 weeks...The baby is born

FETAL POSITIONS AT BIRTH

Locked twins.....Babies' limbs tangled (most difficult position)

Transverse lie...Lying horizontally

Leg presentation...............One leg first (other leg gets stuck)

Arm presentation......................Arms first (shoulders get stuck)

Footling breech...Both legs first

Flexed breech...Bottom first

Cephalic face forward......................................Head first, face up

Cephalic face backward........................Head first, face down (the ideal position)

THE FIVE STEPS OF AMPUTATION

1. Tie off any veins or arteries to reduce blood loss.
2. Cut through the muscles with a knife.
3. Saw through the bone with an electric saw.
4. Pull the skin and muscle flaps over the stump.
5. Attach a mechanical limb as required.

THE PHANTOM LIMB

People who have had a limb amputated often experience sensations such as warmth, cold, itching, squeezing, or burning in that limb, as though it were still present. Phantom pains can also occur in people born without limbs and people who are paralyzed.

> There are more nerve cells in your brain than there are stars in the Milky Way.

WARP SPASM

According to myth, some Celtic heroes were said to grow so angered in battle that their bodies turned inside out. This was known as a "warp spasm." First, the hair on the warrior's body would stand out straight, then a bead of blood would appear on the tip of every hair. Next, the warrior's vital organs would burst out through the skin, pulsating and beating like drums. Finally, a jet of black blood would spurt from the skull. At this point the warrior's enemies would usually flee in fear.

DEAD OR ALIVE?

Hair is dead.
Bones are alive.
Fingernails are dead.
Teeth are alive.

EXTINCT HOMINIDS

Hominids or "Hominidae" lived as far back as 10 million years ago, originating in Africa. Some evolved into humans and some into apes. Most became extinct.

AUSTRALOPHITHECUS AFARENSIS lived 3 million years ago in Ethiopia. A skeleton was found and nicknamed "Lucy" by scientists who, at the time, were listening to the song "Lucy in the Sky with Diamonds" by The Beatles. She was just over 3 ft. 3 in. (100 cm) tall.

HOMO HABILIS means "handy man." He got his name because archaeologists discovered he used simple tools made of wood or flint. He was about 4 ft. 6 in. (140 cm) tall and lived about 2 million years ago in Tanzania.

HOMO ERECTUS lived about 1.8 million years ago. He stood upright at about 5 ft. 9 in. (180 cm) tall. Skeletons have been found all over Europe and Asia, leading scientists to believe that he was the first species to travel out of Africa to colonize other continents.

HOMO NEANDERTHALENSIS or Neanderthal Man was a hunter-gatherer who moved across Europe, the Middle East, and Southwest Asia around 250,000–30,000 years ago. He was short and muscular, and evolved to cope with the extreme cold of the Ice Age. Modern humans (Homo Sapiens) evolved alongside him. No one knows for certain whether Neanderthals died out or if they interbred with modern humans.

HOMO FLORESIENSIS were named after the island Flores in Indonesia, on which a skeleton was discovered in 2003. They lived at least 18,000 years ago and are also known as Hobbits because they were little more than 3 feet (1 meter) tall.

TYPES OF BURNS

DRY BURN
Flames, rope burns, contact with hot objects

ELECTRICAL BURN
Domestic appliances, overhead cables, lightning

SCALD
Steam, hot liquids

RADIATION BURN
Sunburn, x-rays

COLD INJURY
Frostbite, contact with freezing metals or vapors

DEGREES OF BURNS

FIRST DEGREE: skin pink to red, mild swelling, causes pain, takes three to five days to heal. Doesn't often scar.

SECOND DEGREE: skin entirely red, moderate swelling, causes pain and blisters, takes two to six weeks to heal. Often leaves a scar.

THIRD DEGREE: skin white, brown, yellow, or black, severe swelling, no pain after initial burning because nerve cells are damaged, takes many months to heal. Almost always scars.

FOURTH DEGREE: skin blackened, no swelling, no pain after initial burning because nerve cells are damaged. May partly heal, but there is usually permanent damage.

MENTAL ILLNESS IN THE PAST

Until the nineteenth century, people with mental illnesses were not cared for as they are today. Even in hospitals, care for the mentally ill amounted to little more than restraint. Violent patients were chained to the floor or wall. In London, England, paying visitors were invited into Bethlem Royal Hospital to view the inmates, who could be goaded with sticks into behaving oddly or fighting each other.

UNUSUAL MENTAL DISORDERS

LYCANTHROPY

The afflicted person has a delusional belief that he or she is transforming into a wolf.

MUNCHAUSEN'S SYNDROME

The sufferer pretends to have the symptoms of various illnesses in order to receive treatment. The syndrome is named after a fictional character called Baron Munchausen, who used to make up impossible stories of his own adventures.

DE CLERAMBAULT'S SYNDROME

The sufferer is totally convinced that another person is madly in love with them and won't be told otherwise.

AGNOSIA

The afflicted person loses the ability to recognize familiar objects or people, even though there may be nothing wrong with their memory or senses. For example, they might not be able to identify an object such as a frying pan, or the face of their best friend in a crowd.

THE BODY'S REACTION TO BLOOD LOSS

An adult's body contains around 8.7 pints (5 liters) of blood. You can lose some blood without suffering serious effects, but as you lose more, your body goes into a state of shock:

LOSING 1 PINT (0.5 LITERS) OF BLOOD — Little or no effect. This is the quantity normally taken when people donate blood.

LOSING 3.5 PINTS (2 LITERS) OF BLOOD — A hormone called adrenaline is released, making your heart beat faster and your body sweat. The blood vessels in your skin shut down and you look pale. All the remaining blood in your body goes to the vital organs that need to keep working for you to stay alive. You feel weak, shaky, sweaty, and confused; this is known as "shock."

LOSING 5.5 PINTS (3 LITERS) OF BLOOD — Your pulse can no longer be felt in your wrist and you black out. It is possible you will stop breathing and your heart will fail. You may die.

BLOOD GROUPS

There are four main blood groups: A, B, AB, and O. Patients sometimes need to be given blood taken from other people. Your blood group affects who you can give blood to, and who you can receive blood from.

BLOOD TYPE	CAN GIVE TO	CAN RECEIVE FROM
A	A and AB	A and O
B	B and AB	B and O
AB	AB	A, B, AB, and O
O	A, B, AB, and O	O

TYPES OF TEETH

INCISORS
have a single edge for cutting and slicing;
you have eight of these teeth.

CANINES
end in a single, rounded point for gripping and tearing;
you have four of these teeth.

PREMOLARS
have two raised edges for chewing;
children have four of these teeth and adults have eight.

MOLARS
have a flat surface for grinding;
children have four of these teeth and adults have eight,
plus four more "wisdom" teeth later in life.

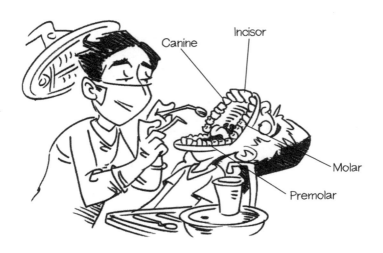

Tooth enamel is the hardest substance
made by the human body.

THE REASON FOR PAIN

When you injure yourself, the sensation of pain lets you know about it so that you can take steps to stop the damage. It also, hopefully, teaches you not to do the same thing again in the future.

During a sporting contest or battle, your body releases natural painkillers, called endorphins, to mask the pain for a short while.

THE SPEED OF PAIN

If you dip your toe into scalding bath water it will hurt and you will speedily remove your foot from the water. The speed at which this happens is the speed at which nerve signals move around your body.

Inside and out, your body is covered with sense receptors called "nocioceptors." When they sense damage, they fire a nerve signal to your spinal cord. There, the signal is understood, and another signal is sent straight back to the muscles to move quickly. At the same time, the spinal cord fires another signal up to the brain, which is understood as pain. Ouch!

It can take longer to actually feel the pain than it does to pull away, so the pain often comes after the response.

EVOLUTION ON EARTH

4.6 billion years ago	The Earth forms
3.5 billion years ago	Single-cell life evolves
555 million years ago	Multi-cell marine life evolves
500 million years ago	Fish evolve
450 million years ago	Land plants evolve
360 million years ago	Vertebrates move onto land
248 million years ago	Virtual extinction of all life
225 million years ago	Dinosaurs evolve
200 million years ago	Mammals and birds evolve
65 million years ago	Extinction of land dinosaurs
3-4 million years ago	Early hominids evolve
130,000 years ago	Modern humans evolve

MEDICAL MACHINES

X-ray machine	Takes photos of bones
Ventilator	Helps with breathing
CAT scanner	Takes images of inside the body
Bypass pump	Takes over for the heart and lungs
Defibrillator	Delivers an electric shock to get the heart beating

PHOBIAS

Having a phobia of something is more than just being afraid of it. Phobias can become irrational, all-consuming, and extreme fears, even when no danger is present.

Arachnophobia..Spiders

Acrophobia..Heights

Claustrophobia..Small spaces

Agoraphobia......................Being out and around other people

Triskaidekaphobia..Number 13

Monophobia...Being alone

Zoophobia..Animals

Neophobia...Anything new

Peladophobia...Bald people

Ablutophobia...Bathing

Taphophobia...Being buried alive

ALLERGIES

The body's self-defense system fights infection. Sometimes, for no reason at all, it attacks harmless substances like pet fur or pollen ("allergens") thinking they pose a danger. When this happens you get an allergic reaction such as swelling, itching, or redness. The most extreme overreaction of the body's defenses is called "anaphylactic shock": your blood pressure drops, your skin, lips, and tongue swell, and you develop a severe asthma attack. It can be life-threatening without a swift injection of adrenaline into your system.

To test for allergies, a few drops of a solution containing an allergen are dripped onto the skin. The skin is then pricked with a needle. If you are allergic to the substance, a red lump will form on the spot within half an hour.

COLORFUL DISEASES

WHITE PLAGUE
Tuberculosis can turn the skin deathly pale.

BLUE HORROR
Cholera can cause such dehydration that the skin turns blue.

YELLOW FEVER
A viral disease that causes liver failure, which leads to a yellowing of the skin.

BLACK DEATH
A symptom of the bubonic plague is dark blotches on the skin.

GANGRENE

Gangrene occurs when a part of your body dies, even though you are still living. It usually starts with the death of cells in the hands or feet caused by infection or a lack of blood flow. This leads to that body part turning black as it decays, and often results in the gangrenous part falling off by itself, or needing to be amputated.

THE ORIGIN OF SPECIES

People were deeply shocked in 1859 when Charles Darwin, a British naturalist, published his theory *On The Origin of Species by Means of Natural Selection*, stating that all living things develop slowly over thousands of years, evolving and adapting to their environment.

MOST PEOPLE THOUGHT...	DARWIN THOUGHT...
...God had created the world exactly as it is today.	...the world has not always been the same as it is now.
...the world was created by God in six days and on the seventh day he rested.	...the world developed slowly over billions of years.
...human beings are both different from and better than all other animals.	...human beings are simply animals that differ only slightly from apes.

The blue flecks on the top of Stilton cheese are mold. The mold gives Stilton its powerful flavor.

When you flush the toilet, thousands of tiny droplets of water, pee, and bits of poo spray into the room.

FECES

The scientific name for poo, the smelly brown waste product of digestion, is "feces." Feces is made up of all the leftover stuff that your body can't or doesn't need to digest, such as dead cells, salt, mucus, intestinal juices, water, and bacteria, as well as the odd bit of fruit peel and fiber.

You excrete around 100 billion bacteria every day. More than half of your solid waste is thought to be bacteria. There are more than 75 different kinds of bacteria in feces.

You produce 2-7 oz. (65-200 g) of feces per day.

"Indole" and "skatole" are the chemicals responsible for making feces smell so bad.

If you have an excessive amount of gas in your stomach, you have "flatulence." The gas is formed by bacteria that help digest your food. When the gas arrives at your rectum you let it out as a fart.

Humans fart an average of 14 times a day.

Talking while taking a poo is a bit of a strain. When you push with your stomach muscles, your voice box automatically closes. Anything you say at this moment sounds like an impression of an old rock star.

FART-TASTIC FOODS
Brussels sprouts • Cabbage • Cauliflower
Fizzy drinks • Prunes • Brown bread
Baked beans • Onions • Bran

HUMAN GUINEA PIGS

VACCINATION

Dr. Edward Jenner noticed that people who had had cowpox (a relatively harmless disease) didn't catch the deadly smallpox. In 1796, he tested his theory on eight-year-old James Phipps. Jenner injected Phipps with cowpox pus in one arm and the boy broke out in a fever, but soon recovered. Jenner then injected him with smallpox and no disease followed.

CHLOROFORM

The nineteenth-century Scottish doctor, James Young Simpson, investigated the effects of chloroform on his dinner guests, who fell unconscious and slipped under the dining room table. He went on to be the first doctor to use chloroform as a painkiller during childbirth, for which he was knighted. "Victo Dolore" is the inscription of his coat of arms. It means, "pain conquered."

BLOOD TRANSFUSION

In 1667, the French royal physician Jean-Baptiste Denys injected the blood of a sheep into a sick boy, who recovered. He then did the same with other patients, but one died and Denys was tried for murder. Blood transfusions were stopped until new discoveries made the practice safer.

PENICILLIN

In 1941, a policeman in Oxford, England, cut himself shaving and the wound became infected with staphylococci and streptococci bacteria, which entered the blood. He had a fever of 105°F (40.5°C) and oozing boils on his face. For five days the policeman was given penicillin. The fever went and the boils cleared up, but on the last day the supply of the drug ran out, and the policeman eventually died.

WHERE BATHROOM GERMS LIVE

Down the toilet • The sink overflow

The prickles of your toothbrush • Bars of soap

Between the fibers of your towels • The faucets

Under the shower mat • The doorknob

BAD PERSONAL HYGIENE

Let your hair get really greasy and smelly.

Never brush your teeth.

Don't wash your hands after going to the toilet.

Spray everything with spit when you sneeze or cough.

Pick your nose often.

Multiple bee, wasp, or hornet stings
can cause a deadly allergic reaction.

THE HUMAN LIGHTNING CONDUCTOR

Roy C. Sullivan of the United States has been struck
by lightning no less than seven times.

1942...He lost a big toenail

1969...He lost both eyebrows

1970...His left shoulder was burned

1972...His hair caught fire

1973................His legs were burned and his hair was singed

1976..His ankle was injured

1977....................................His stomach and chest were burned

WHICH IS WORSE?

1. An ice-cream headache.
2. A mouth ulcer.
3. A paper cut.

HOW TO CURE HICCUPS

Hold your breath and count to ten.

Breathe slowly and deeply into a paper bag.

Pull your tongue.

Drink from the far side of a cup.

Clap your hands just before the hiccup.

Try to make yourself sneeze—a sneeze beats a hiccup.

Bend forward so that your head is between your legs,
then have an upside-down drink of water.

Ask one of your friends to try to give you a fright that
will make you jump.

THE FIRST SUCCESSFUL TRANSPLANTS

Kidney...1954, Boston, USA

Liver...1963, Denver, USA

Heart..1967, Cape Town, South Africa

Face...2005, Amiens, France

The recipient of the first successful face transplant had been mauled by a dog. Her new face does not look like that of her donor or her old self—it looks like a cross between the two.

SWAPPING BODY PARTS

In Mary Shelley's book *Frankenstein*, a crazed doctor stitches together a patchwork man with body parts stolen from the local graveyard, dissecting rooms, and slaughter houses. To bring the body to life, the mad scientist harnesses energy from a bolt of lightning.

Bacteria are so small that you can fit up to 10,000 of them on your thumbnail. They multiply every 20 minutes or so by splitting in half. That means that in twelve hours one bacterium can produce more than 34 billion copies of itself.

DEADLY INFECTIONS, PAST AND PRESENT

PLAGUE
Plague is spread from one rat to another by fleas that then bite and infect humans. In the Middle Ages, the bubonic plague killed about a third of the population of Europe.

RABIES
Caught from the bite or scratch of an infected animal, rabies affects the brain and causes insanity if left untreated. It blocks the nerve signals that cause swallowing, causing spit infected with the virus to dribble out of the mouth.

POLIO
Symptoms include fever, fatigue, headache, vomiting, stiffness in the neck, and pain in the limbs. One in 200 infections leads to irreversible paralysis. Five to ten percent of people die when the muscles that control their breathing become paralyzed.

HIV
HIV is the virus that causes AIDS (Acquired Immune Deficiency Syndrome), a disease that destroys the body's ability to fight infection. Since 1985, almost 22 million people have died from AIDS.

SMALLPOX
Causes bumps to form on the skin that then turn into hard, pus-filled blisters. These then crust over, form scabs, and fall off. This sometimes fatal disease is untreatable, but you can be vaccinated against it.

FLU
Spread by droplets of spit. In 1918, a deadly strain of flu that could kill a person within 48 hours, killed between 20 million and 50 million people. New strains of flu appear when previous strains of the virus mutate.

WHAT'S SNOT AND WHAT'S NOT?

Snot is a mucus that is secreted from the inside of your nose and small holes in your skull called "sinuses."

Snot protects your body from invaders such as germs, pollen, and dust. It traps these invaders like wasps in jam so that they can't reach your lungs.

Snot is mostly water. It also contains a dash of salt and a sugary protein called "mucin."

SUCK OUT THE SNOT

The Basotho people of Lesotho in southern Africa use a small metal implement for picking their noses, and loving mothers suck the snot from their babies' noses.

NOSE PICKING

"Pick 'em, lick 'em, roll 'em, flick 'em."

"Got you, squashed you, now I'm going to eat you."

"You can pick your friends and you can pick your nose, but you can't pick your friend's nose."

"What's the difference between boogers and broccoli? I won't eat broccoli."

BLOODSUCKERS

Mosquitoes • Leeches • Horseflies • Sandflies
Vampire bats • Head lice • Lamprey fish • Ticks

THE KISS OF A VAMPIRE

There are three species of vampire bats. All of them are found in central and southern America. By day, they roost in caves and mines, then at night they emerge to feed on the blood of other animals.

Vampire bats have a chemical in their saliva that stops their victim's blood from clotting. This allows them to drink for as long as they want. The chemical is called "draculin," after the bloodsucking Count Dracula.

If a vampire bat can't get its nightly feed of blood, it doesn't go hungry. It flies back to the cave and asks another well-fed bat for a blood donation. The bats lock mouths and the blood trickles between them. It looks like they are kissing.

It is said that in 453 A.D. the bloodthirsty warlord Attila the Hun died of a nosebleed on his wedding night.

WHY WE NEED VITAMINS AND MINERALS

Vitamin A...Eyes, skin, immune system
(carrots, cheese)

Vitamin B............................Energy, blood, nervous system, skin
(yeast, whole grains,
milk, fish, meat, eggs)

Vitamin C..................Immune system, tendons, ligaments, skin
(citrus fruits, potatoes)

Vitamin D...Bones and teeth
(eggs, milk, sunlight)

Vitamin E.........................Immune system, nervous system, skin
(green vegetables, nuts)

Iron...Red blood cells
(red meats, green vegetables)

Calcium..Bones and teeth
(milk, yogurt, cheese)

Zinc...Enzymes, immune system
(green vegetables, cheese, seeds)

GROWING

Your eyes stop growing when you are about seven
or eight years old.

During your lifetime your nails will grow
a total of about 9 feet (2.8 m).

Your ears and nose keep growing throughout your life.

GIGANTISM

This is a medical condition in which the pituitary gland, which produces growth hormones, goes into overdrive. People with this condition don't just grow upward. They also tend to develop thick and heavy bones, a heavy jaw, and large hands and feet. Typically, a pituitary giant reaches 7–8 ft. (210–240 cm).

The tallest man in medical history was Robert Pershing Wadlow of the United States. He grew to be 8 ft. 11 in. (272 cm) tall.

DWARFISM

This is a genetic condition that affects not only humans, but also animals and plants. Dwarfism prevents the sufferer from reaching the normal size for the species. In humans it often makes parts of the body grow out of proportion. Typically, an adult dwarf grows no taller than 4 ft. 4 in. (130 cm) tall.

The shortest mature human was Gul Mohammed of India. He measured 22.5 in. (57 cm) tall.

As you grow taller, your center of gravity shifts. If this happens too quickly (which it often does during puberty) your brain can't keep up. A period of clumsiness is unavoidable.

THE SKELETON

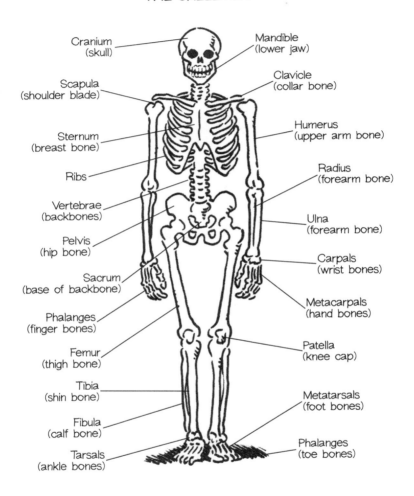

Cranium
(skull)

Mandible
(lower jaw)

Scapula
(shoulder blade)

Clavicle
(collar bone)

Sternum
(breast bone)

Humerus
(upper arm bone)

Ribs

Radius
(forearm bone)

Vertebrae
(backbones)

Ulna
(forearm bone)

Pelvis
(hip bone)

Carpals
(wrist bones)

Sacrum
(base of backbone)

Metacarpals
(hand bones)

Phalanges
(finger bones)

Femur
(thigh bone)

Patella
(knee cap)

Tibia
(shin bone)

Metatarsals
(foot bones)

Fibula
(calf bone)

Phalanges
(toe bones)

Tarsals
(ankle bones)

Bone is regularly renewed by your body. It takes around seven years to make the equivalent of a new skeleton.

HOW TO EXERCISE YOUR MUSCLES

You should exercise your muscles every day, but never try to do too much at one time.

DELTOID (shoulders)
Lie flat on your stomach and position your hands on the floor underneath your shoulders. Keeping your toes on the floor, push the rest of your body up with your arms. This is called a "push-up."

PECTORALIS MAJOR (chest)
Ask a friend to bend his arms at the elbows and put them up in front of him. Now adopt the same position, with your arms outside your friend's so that his are between yours. Try to push your friend's arms together while he tries to push yours apart.

BICEPS (top of arm)
With a weight in your hand, curl your arm like you are flexing your muscle.

RECTUS ABDOMINIS (stomach)
Lie flat on your back with your knees raised and your hands at the side of your head. Now use your stomach

muscles to raise your shoulders off the floor until you feel the strain, then lie back down, without actually touching the floor. This is called a "sit-up."

QUADRICEPS (front of thigh)
Stand with your back against a wall, then bend to a sitting position. Hold, and then straighten up again. This is called a "deep-knee bend."

GLUTEUS MAXIMUS (bottom)
Lie flat on your stomach. Keeping your legs straight, lift them as far as you can off the floor. Put your hands on your buttocks so you can feel them tighten.

HOW MANY LEGS?

Human	2
Dog	4
Insect	6
Spider	8
Centipede	30–100
Millipede	80–750

HOW TO MAKE FAKE BLOOD

1. Place two spoonfuls of golden syrup in a cup.
2. Stir in one spoonful of water.
3. Stir in two drops of red food coloring.
4. Add a pinch of chocolate powder.
5. Drip the fake blood from the corners of your mouth.
6. Try to spook your friends. This is best done on Halloween.

BODY INTRUDERS

VIRUSES

Description: Nasty-looking chemical packages, that have protein coatings and can be spiky.

Size: Range from 20–250 nanometers long (microscopic).

Mission: To take over your cells so that they can reproduce and invade other cells.

Most wanted: Polio, HIV, Flu, and the common cold.

BACTERIA

Description: Single-celled organisms shaped like short rods, spheres, or spirals. Contain all the genetic information needed to make copies of themselves. Some have threadlike paddles ("flagella") that they use to move around.

Size: At least 1 micrometer (0.001 mm) long (100 times larger than viruses) (microscopic).

Mission: To reproduce, often making toxins that damage cells.

Most wanted: The Black Death, MRSA.

FUNGI

Description: Molds, yeasts, and mushrooms.

Size: From 0.01 mm to as large as a mushroom.

Mission: To cause infection—but some, such as penicillin, kill harmful bacteria in your body.

Most wanted: Candida, Athlete's Foot.

WORMS

Description: Wriggling parasites.

Size: From microscopic to up to about 30 feet (9 m) long.

Mission: To live off nutrients in your intestine, lungs, liver, skin, or brain.

Most wanted: Tapeworms and roundworms.

THE BARBER-SURGEONS OF FLEET STREET

For centuries, surgery was a craft rather than a profession. In England, surgery was often performed by barbers. As well as providing a shampoo and blow-dry, barbers were also handy with a scalpel. Once in the chair, customers would be asked if they wanted a short back and sides, a little off the top, or perhaps a tooth extraction and some loss of blood. The barbershop's red-and-white striped pole goes back to these times. The red represents the blood and the white represents the "tourniquet" (a bandage or rope used to slow down the blood flow).

HOW TO MAKE FAKE SNOT

1. Heat a spoonful of golden syrup and green jelly in the microwave for just ten seconds.
2. Add a few drops of green food coloring.
3. Pour on a handkerchief and fake an enormous sneeze.
4. Show to horrified witnesses.

THE SIGNS OF OLD AGE

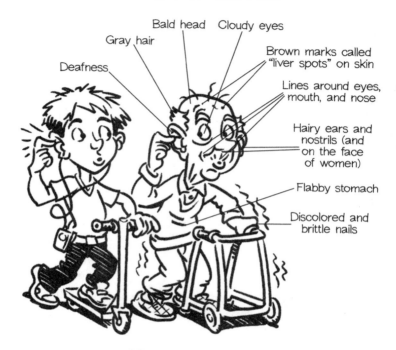

Gray hair
Bald head · Cloudy eyes
Deafness
Brown marks called "liver spots" on skin
Lines around eyes, mouth, and nose
Hairy ears and nostrils (and on the face of women)
Flabby stomach
Discolored and brittle nails

GROWTH SPURTS

Girls tend to shoot up between the ages of 12 and 13, and stop growing at 18 years old. Boys usually grow fastest between the ages of 14 and 15, and finish growing when they reach 20 years old. This is what happens during a growth spurt:

1. Hands and feet get bigger.
2. Shin bones and forearms lengthen.
3. Thigh bones and upper arms grow.
4. Spine extends.
5. Shoulders and chest broaden in boys; hips and pelvis widen in girls.

HUMAN VITAL STATISTICS

Pancreas..3-4 oz. (85-115 g)

Spleen..4 oz. (115 g)

Kidneys..6 oz. (170 g) each

Heart..1 lb. (0.5 kg)

Lungs..1 lb. (0.5 kg) each

Brain..3 lb. (1.4 kg)

Liver...4 lb. (2 kg)

Blood..11 lb. (5 kg)

Skin..20 square feet (6 square meters)

Intestines..25 ft. (7.5 m) long

Muscles account for about 42% of the total body weight
in men and 36% in women.

HYPNOSIS

Hypnosis is a way of putting someone into a relaxed and
focused state, in which the hypnotist can access the
person's subconscious mind.

Entertainers sometimes use hypnotism to make people do
amusing things that they might not normally do in public.
Therapists can use hypnotism to try to help people give
up smoking, cure their eczema, or overcome an irrational
fear of spiders.

Some detectives use hypnosis to help people
remember details of crimes or even events that
took place years in the past.

Find out whether you would be a good candidate for
hypnosis by opening your eyes wide and rolling them
upward, then lowering your eyelids without rolling your
eyes downward again. It is said that if you can do this
task you are likely to be easy to hypnotize.

NERVES

Nerves carry messages to and from your brain. They spread and divide throughout your body, like telephone cables. They link every single part of your body with your brain and spinal cord, and signals flash up and down them at about 164-197 feet (50-60 m) per second.

Nerves run together in bundles of thousands. They are very delicate and so most of them are buried deep within your body, out of harm's way. When they run near the surface of the skin, you need to watch out. The ulna nerve that runs down your arm to your wrist and fingers, for example, is vulnerable at the elbow. When you hit this nerve, or "funny bone," a tingling sensation shoots down your arm.

ASEXUAL REPRODUCTION

In asexual reproduction, a single individual produces offspring that are genetically identical to itself:

Fission..............................The single-celled parent splits in two
(Bacteria, paramecium)

Budding..Offspring grows from a bud on
(Hydras, spider plants)   the parent's body

Gemule.......................................A bud of cells inside the parent
(Freshwater sponges)   grows into a new organism

Fragmentation..............The parent breaks into pieces, each
(Flatworms)   of which can produce an offspring

Regeneration...................................A detached piece of parent
(Starfish, sea cucumbers)   grows into a new individual

Parthenogenesis...The parent produces eggs that develop
(Honey bees, lizards)   into offspring without fertilization

CAPITAL PUNISHMENT

The Latin word for head is *caput* or *capitis*. The terms
"capital offense," "capital crime," and "capital punishment"
derive from the Roman punishment for serious
offenses—the removal of the head.

During the French Revolution (1789-99), thousands of
French aristocrats had their heads chopped off. It was
common practice for the executioner to hold up the
severed head toward the excited crowds. It was believed
that the head could still see for around ten seconds
after it was chopped off.

The last words uttered by Queen Marie
Antoinette of France were "Excuse me, Sir"
when she stepped on her executioner's foot.

According to ancient folklore, a
drink taken from the skull of a
hanged man will cure all ills.

THE ANATOMY OF THE BRAIN

Different parts of the human brain perform different
functions and make us who we are:

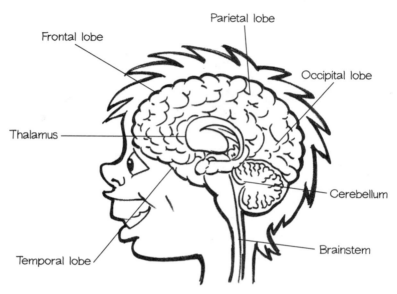

FRONTAL LOBE — Influences personality, judgment, abstract reasoning, social behavior, and language.

PARIETAL LOBE — Regulates perception of touch, pressure, temperature, and pain.

OCCIPITAL LOBE — Relates to vision.

TEMPORAL LOBE — Relates to hearing and memory.

THALAMUS — Receives sensory information.

BRAINSTEM — Controls breathing, digestion, heart rate, and blood pressure.

CEREBELLUM — Regulates balance, movement, and muscle coordination.

TYPES OF MEMORY

Your brain stores millions of kinds of memories. Your short-term memory, or "working" memory, holds memories such as where you put your bag, or reminds you to do your homework, and these are usually forgotten after a short time. However, some information—often things that are emotionally important, such as opening your birthday presents, or memories that are useful to your survival, like remembering that hot water will scald you—passes into your long-term memory, where it stays for days, weeks, or even your whole life.

IMPROVING YOUR MEMORY

Your memory for facts can be improved dramatically by associating images with things you want to remember, or by using "mnemonics." Mnemonics are sentences or words that hold memory clues.

The mnemonic *"Richard Of York Gave Battle In Vain,"* for example, can be used to help remember the order of colors in the rainbow because the first letter of each word corresponds to a color: Red, Orange, Yellow, Green, Blue, Indigo, Violet.

Associations can, however, lead to false memories. If you've seen several images or a list of words (for example: "pencil," "crayon," "paint"), you might think you "remember" a related word that was not in the list (such as "paintbrush").

The brain weighs about 3 lbs. (1.4 kg) and accounts for 2% of the average body mass. It looks like an oversized walnut.

WHAT HAPPENS WHEN YOU SWEAT

1. Your brain registers that you are hot, scared, or nervous.

2. Sweat glands produce a mixture of water and salts.

3. The sweat travels through a tube, called a duct, to the skin.

4. Heat from your body is transferred to the sweat.

5. The heat increases the speed of the water molecules in the sweat, making them evaporate into the air and cooling you down.

6. The sodium and potassium salts in the sweat are left behind on your skin, which is why it tastes salty.

TOUCH

Your sense of touch comes from millions of sense receptors in your skin. Some of these receptors can feel the lightest touch, while others feel harder pressure, or temperature. There are concentrations of sense receptors in sensitive parts of the skin like the fingertips, or around the roots of hairs.

ANIMALS THAT CAN REGROW BODY PARTS

A lizard can regrow a severed tail.

Some species of starfish can regrow lost arms. A few can regrow the rest of the starfish from a severed arm.

Salamanders can regrow entire limbs.

Flatworms, if cut in half, will regenerate into two functioning flatworms.

WHEN YOU ARE SCARED

When you are scared your body releases the
hormone "adrenaline" (epinephrine), which causes
the following responses:

Pupils widen.................................to help you see more clearly

Hair stands on end.......................to make you more sensitive

Breathing rate increases.....to increase your oxygen intake

Sweating..................................to cool your overworked system

Body releases endorphins............................to counteract pain

Skin goes pale.........................to limit blood loss and redirect
blood to your essential organs

Heart rate increases..................to pump more blood to your
muscles and brain

One way of cooling down in a hot
country is to eat spicy food such as
curry or chili. This causes sweating,
particularly on the face, which then
evaporates, cooling the skin.

RIDING A ROLLER COASTER

THE TENSE WAIT: You climb into your seat. The head-and-shoulder restraint comes down over your head. You feel a little nervous.

THE SLOW CLIMB: Your heart beats faster. Your breathing becomes shallow and fast. The hormone adrenaline floods your body, triggering an instinctive "fight or flight" response. But there is no turning back.

THE BIG DOWN: You are slammed into your seat by the gravitational force. It is difficult to lift your hands, head, or feet. Everything is heavy. Your heart has to beat harder to pump the blood around your body. Your brain does not get enough oxygen and you feel dizzy.

THE 180° TURN: Your head gets very heavy and, if you don't strain to keep it forward, it hits the guard like a clapper in a bell. If you were to continue at this rate of acceleration for more than a couple of seconds you would experience tunnel vision, followed by gravity-induced loss of consciousness, known as "g-LOC" or "blackout."

THE HIGH-SPEED HILL: As you go up the hill your head

momentarily clears. Then you hit the crest. You feel light-headed. Your body strains to lift out of the seat. Blood rushes to your head. You feel its pressure behind your eyes. Too much of this and your vision will turn red, known as "red-out."

THE LOOP: You are pressed down into your seat. The extra weight on your legs, lap, and shoulders stops you from feeling like you're upside-down.

THE END: You slow down. You have survived a near-death experience. Your body is pumped with adrenaline. Euphoria kicks in. Do you want to go again?

TIPS FOR LOOKING BIG AND SCARY

It is thought that one of the reasons our hair stands on end when we are frightened is to make us look big and scary. Some animals are better at this than we are:

The Australian Frilled lizard has a flap of loose skin around its neck that can expand like a huge collar.

When certain butterflies are scared they open their wings to reveal two large spots that look like the eyes of a much bigger animal.

The Goliath Bird-Eating spider makes a hissing noise by rubbing bristles on its legs together. It also rears up on its hind legs to scare off predators.

Although huge, bison aren't quite as big as they first look. Their beards give them a lot of extra padding.

DISEASE-CARRYING INSECTS

Cockroaches • Harvest mites • Ticks
Black flies • Mosquitoes • Tsetse flies

SEXUAL REPRODUCTION

The embryo from which a human baby develops is created when an egg from a female is fertilized by a spermatozoon from a male. The fertilization process takes place as a result of sexual intercourse, during which a human male inserts his erect penis into a woman's vagina and ejaculates millions of spermatozoon cells. The "sperm" make their way toward the egg, and the first sperm to reach the egg fertilizes it. The embryo then imbeds itself in the wall of the uterus, and begins its growth into a baby.

PRIMARY REPRODUCTIVE ORGANS

MALE: Penis, Testes
Sperm are produced in vast numbers in the testicles from puberty onward. Up to 200 million may form per day, which is around 1,500 per second. Any that are not released are broken down and reabsorbed by the body.

FEMALE: Ovaries, Uterus, Fallopian tubes, Vagina
All the ova (eggs) that a woman has are present in her ovaries at birth. From puberty, one egg ripens every month and is released into the uterus. The lining of the uterus thickens, in readiness for an egg. If the egg is fertilized by a sperm, the resulting embryo embeds itself in the uterus lining. If the egg is not fertilized then it, along with the lining of the uterus, is shed through the vagina during menstruation. This is commonly known as a "period."

DON'T LOSE YOUR HEAD!

During sex, the female praying mantis sometimes eats
the male, starting with the head. Oddly, scientists have
discovered that about ten minutes after losing his head
the decapitated male mantis' sexual performance
actually improves.

SEXUAL REPRODUCTION IN ANIMALS

Both male and female birds have an opening to the body
called a "cloaca." Mating birds press their cloacas together
and sperm moves from the male to the female. It happens
quickly. Swifts can even mate in flight.

The male scorpion produces his sperm in a small packet,
which he leaves on the ground. He leads the female over
the sperm, so that a small hook on the packet attaches
to her genital opening. The sperm can then enter her
body and fertilize her eggs.

Female salmon lay eggs into a shallow pit in the riverbed.
The male sheds sperm over them and the female covers
the eggs with pebbles or gravel.

If you are "steatopygous" you have
a big, fatty bottom.

A FAMOUS FAT MAN

Daniel Lambert was born on March 13, 1770. As a young man of 5 ft. 11 in. (181 cm), he is said to have eaten and drunk only in moderation. At age 23 he weighed 447 lbs. (203 kg) and at age 34 he weighed 667 lbs. (303 kg). He had to have his clothes and furniture specially made to fit. This cost a lot of money, so he toured England in a custom-made carriage and charged people a small fee to look at "England's fattest man." In 1809 he died suddenly, at age 39, weighing 737 lbs. (335 kg).

The heaviest man in history was Jon
Brower Minnoch of the United States
(1941–83). At his heaviest, he is thought
to have weighed 1400 lbs. (635 kg).

THE THREE TYPES OF MUSCLES

SKELETAL (OR VOLUNTARY) muscles are used to move the body. You can contract and relax them at will.

SMOOTH (OR INVOLUNTARY) muscle is found in the walls of the internal organs such as the intestines. You can't consciously control them.

CARDIAC muscle forms the wall of the heart. It automatically contracts around 100,000 times a day.

The quickest muscles in the
body are found in the eye.

MAJOR MUSCLES

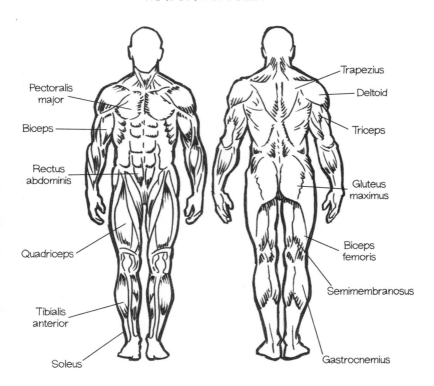

The body's smallest muscle, called the "stapedius," prevents the tiny bones in your ear from being shaken too much by loud noises.

Sound does not just travel through air. Surprisingly, sound travels through solids and liquids faster than it does through air. This allows some marine life to communicate over vast distances.

THE EYE

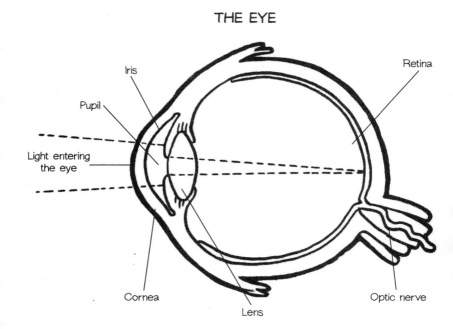

HOW YOUR EYES WORK

As light rays enter your eye, they are bent and focused
by the lens and cornea to form an image on the retina
at the back of your eye. This process, however, flips the
image upside-down. It is your brain's job to flip it again
so that it is the right way up. In fact, if you wore special
glasses that inverted the light rays before they hit your
eyes, so that they arrived on your retina the right way
up, your brain would flip it over, realize its mistake,
then flip it back again.

The pattern of colors on your iris is unique, and
iris scans are increasingly used to check people's
identity, like taking a fingerprint.

THE IRIS

The colorful bit of your eye is called the iris. Your iris might be brown, blue, hazel, or green, but it is not just for show. It is in fact a ring of muscle. When there is a lot of light, the iris reacts to make the black pupil in the middle smaller and reduce the amount of light that can enter the eye. In poor light, the iris opens the pupil to let in as much light as possible.

CAT EYES

Cats can see in the dark because they have a mirrorlike membrane at the back of their eyes called a "tapetum." This membrane reflects light back through the seeing-cells of the eye a second time, giving them another chance to absorb every "photon," or molecule, of light.

VISUAL IMPAIRMENTS

NEAR-SIGHTED	FAR-SIGHTED	ASTIGMATISM
Trouble focusing on objects in the distance.	Trouble focusing on things close up.	Trouble focusing on things both in the distance and close up.
Light rays from distant objects meet at a point in front of the retina.	Light rays from nearby objects meet at a point behind the retina.	Light rays do not meet, but instead scatter.
Eyeball is too long or cornea is too curved.	Eyeball is too short or cornea is not curved enough.	Cornea is oval like a football rather than round like a soccer ball.

DON'T SWEAT IT

The milk produced by female mammals is actually a type of sweat. This means that when you drink a glass of milk, you are actually drinking cow's sweat.

ALTITUDE SICKNESS

Altitude sickness is the body's reaction to a lack of oxygen at high altitudes—around 5,000 ft. (1,500 m) above sea level or above. To avoid it mountain climbers try not to sleep at altitudes 1,000 ft. (300 m) higher than they had the night before. This means if they climb 1,640 ft. (500 m) in a day, they must descend 660 ft. (200 m) before making camp.

Early symptoms: Drowsiness and weakness during physical exertion.

Severe symptoms: Headache, insomnia, persistent rapid pulse, nausea, and vomiting.

Extreme symptoms:
Confusion, psychosis, hallucinations, persistent coughing.

Finally: Seizures, coma, and death.

FALLING OUT OF YOUR SPACESHIP
WITHOUT A SPACESUIT

One second: Saliva on your tongue evaporates and your eyes dry out.

Three seconds: Your skin is severely sunburned.

Ten seconds: Your joints ache and nitrogen bubbles form in your blood.

Fifteen seconds: Your lungs collapse.

Two minutes: You die.

TERMINAL VELOCITY

Terminal velocity is the speed that a falling object reaches when the resistance of the air (or other substance it is falling through) stops it from accelerating further. If you jumped out of an airplane you would reach a terminal velocity of about 120 mph (195 km/h). If you adopted a diving pose this could increase to about 200 mph (320 km/h). That's the same speed as a peregrine falcon diving down on its prey.

LOUDNESS

Loudness is measured in decibels (dB)

10dB	A human breathing
50dB	Normal conversation
80dB	Busy traffic
108dB	The loudest-ever finger-snap
118.1dB	The loudest-ever burp
120dB	A rock concert
129dB	The loudest-ever scream
150dB	A jet engine
250dB	Inside a tornado (death to humans)

Nightclubbers and concertgoers often experience a high-pitched ringing sound in their ears when they get home. Ringing ears, otherwise known as "tinnitus," occurs when very loud sounds damage the nerves that connect the ear to the brain.

PITCH

If you put your fingers on your throat and make a sound, you can feel the vibrations in your throat. The higher the pitch, the faster the vibrations. The speed at which something vibrates is called the frequency, which is measured in "hertz" (Hz). The lowest sound most people can hear is about 20 Hz. Children's ears can pick up higher frequencies than adults. Some animals, like dogs and bats, can pick up sound frequencies that are too high for human ears to detect.

HEARING IN STEREO

If a sound comes from the side, it reaches one ear a split second before the other and is slightly louder in the first ear. Your brain picks up these tiny differences so that you know, without looking, where a sound is coming from.

ULTRASOUND

Ultrasound has a frequency higher than humans can hear.

Some dog whistles use ultrasound, and though they are silent to human ears, dogs come running.

Bats bounce ultrasonic sounds off objects and listen to the echoes to locate and identify them, including flying prey. It means they don't have to see to be expert flyers.

INFRASOUND

Infrasound has a frequency lower than humans can hear.

Sperm whales use powerful blasts of inaudible infrasound to stun their prey.

It is thought that infrasonic waves emitted from natural disasters such as avalanches, earthquakes, and volcanoes give animals early warning of an approaching disaster.

THE HAND

Primates are the only animals that have hands. Other animals may have paws or claws. A human hand has five digits attached to a broad palm. The names of the digits are:

Thumb

Index finger (or forefinger)

Middle finger

Ring finger

Little finger (or pinky)

You have a flexible, "opposable" thumb that can be used against your four fingers to grasp and hold on to things. Your hand can be trained to do delicate and complicated tasks, such as painting, knitting, typing, and playing musical instruments. Your hand can also form a fighting fist.

> Shridhar Chillal of India has not cut the nails on his left hand since 1952. The total length of his five nails is about 21 feet (6.15 m). His hand is permanently disfigured from supporting the weight of the nails for over 50 years.

CHIROGNOMY

"Chirognomy" is the study of the shape and size of the hand as an indicator of personality.

Long palm, short fingers............................Intuitive and impulsive

Long palm, long fingers..........................Emotional and sensitive

Square palm, short fingers........................Practical and reliable

Square palm, long fingers...........Quick-witted and intellectual

102

REFLEXOLOGY

According to an alternative medicine called "reflexology," you can treat different parts of the body by applying pressure to special points on the soles of the feet:

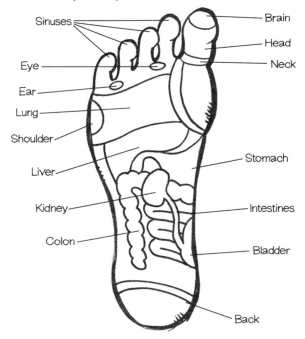

ACUPUNCTURE

Acupuncture involves sticking needles into certain points on the body to help prevent or treat illness. It has been practiced in China and the Far East for thousands of years. It is believed that energy or "qi" (pronounced *chee*) flows through the body along pathways. When a pathway becomes blocked, the patient feels unwell. The needle prick helps to clear the pathway and keep the patient healthy.

THE FOUR HUMORS

Up until the nineteenth century, it was believed that within every person there were four fluids or "humors" that needed to be kept in balance for a person to stay healthy. These were:

Black bile • Yellow bile • Phlegm • Blood

A person known for selfless acts of bravery, for instance, was thought to have a lot of blood in his or her system. Too much black bile led to a gloomy frame of mind. Too much yellow bile caused aggressive behavior. And too much phlegm was believed to make you cold and unemotional.

MANDRAKE

The mandrake is a mythical plant, but this didn't stop other plants being sold as mandrake to gullible people in the Middle Ages. Mixed with small doses of hemlock and opium, it was said to be a highly effective painkiller. According to myth, the roots of the plant resembled a human form and if you tried to uproot it, the hideous sound of its screams would kill you instantly.

WHAT TO DO WITH A SEVERED LIMB

1. Wrap the severed body part in gauze or soft fabric, then place the package in a plastic bag. Place that bag in another bag filled with crushed ice. DO NOT wash the severed part or allow it to come into direct contact with the ice.

2. Clearly mark the package with the time of injury and the person's name.

3. Hand it personally to the doctor (if you have a hand).

DO-IT-YOURSELF AMPUTATION

In 2003, a 27-year-old American called Aron Ralston was forced to cut off his own arm to save his life. He had been hiking in the Bluejohn Canyon in Utah when a 792 lb. (360 kg) rock fell on him and trapped his arm. He was eight miles from his car in a remote area with hardly any food or water. Days passed and no one came to his rescue. On the morning of the fifth day, he took the brave decision to free himself. He tied a rope around his biceps to slow down the flow of blood, and slowly sliced through his arm below the elbow using his pocket knife. The worst part was breaking the bone and cutting through the nerves. The muscle came away surprisingly easily. He then hiked out to meet rescuers.

TYPES OF BODY PIERCING

Nostril • Septum (between the nostrils) • Eyebrow
Eyelid • Tongue • Tongue frenulum (under the tongue)
Nipple • Navel • Bridge of nose • Cheek • Lip

> Elaine Davidson of Scotland holds the world record for the most number of body piercings. She has 720.

SMOKING

Cigarettes contain an addictive substance called "nicotine." That's why when many people start to smoke they find it difficult to give up. Nicotine is a powerful drug that affects the mind as well as the body. The negative effects of smoking are only minor at first and include coughing, smelly breath, and yellow teeth. These side effects usually go away when you stop. People who become addicted to nicotine and continue to smoke often develop more serious illnesses as they become more susceptible to chest infections and breathing problems. The chemicals in tobacco can cause a breakdown of healthy body tissues, and this can lead to fatal illnesses such as heart disease and lung cancer.

KIDNEYS

Your kidneys are located, one on either side, in your lower back. Your kidneys perform three main functions:

1. The removal of urea. Urea is a waste product that is created when the body breaks down proteins. It is diluted with water in the kidneys, then sent to the bladder to be passed out of the body as urine.

2. The adjustment of salt levels. Excess sodium or other salts taken into the body from food are removed from the bloodstream by the kidneys.

3. Balancing your body's water content. The water level of your body must be kept stable in order for you to function well. Of the water you consume as part of food or drink, some is lost as sweat and some in your breath, but most is removed by your kidneys and becomes urine.

THE LIFE CYCLE OF TEETH

6 months: "milk" teeth start to poke through your gums.

2 years: your 20 "milk" teeth are fully grown.

6 years: your "milk" teeth are pushed out, one by one, by the permanent teeth growing behind them.

13 years: your 28 permanent teeth are fully grown.

20 years: four more teeth called "wisdom teeth" grow at the back of your mouth.

70+ years: your teeth start to fall out as your gums weaken.

FALSE TEETH

Poor people used to sell their teeth to rich people who were in need of replacements. If there were no poor people available, human teeth were instead pulled from the mouths of corpses.

THE LIVER

Your liver is your largest internal organ. It performs many important functions, including:

Controlling blood sugar by absorbing excess "glucose," which it stores as "glycogen." If your blood sugar level drops, your liver then converts the glycogen back into glucose, and releases it into your blood.

Converting fats into forms that can be used and stored.

Storing vitamins and minerals.

Producing bile for use in digestion.

Breaking down proteins so they can be used by the body.

Removing hormones from the blood.

Removing and breaking down toxic substances.

Removing bacteria and old blood cells.

Producing proteins needed for blood clotting.

ENZYMES

"Enzymes" are molecules that speed up the rate of chemical reactions in the body. Among other things, they are used in digestion to break down your chewed food into much smaller molecules that your body can absorb:

AMYLASE is an enzyme in "saliva" that breaks down starch (bread, pasta, potato) into sugars such as glucose that can be used for energy.

PROTEASE is an enzyme that breaks down proteins (fish, meat, soya) into "amino acids" that are used as the building blocks for your body.

LIPASE is an enzyme that breaks down fats (seed oils, dairy products) into fatty acids and "glycerol" that can be used for energy.

BREATHING

You have two lungs inside your chest, one on either side of your heart. When you breathe in, air enters through your nose and mouth, goes down your windpipe ("trachea"), then splits down two branches called "bronchi," one going to each lung.

Inside the lung, the air splits and travels into smaller and smaller tubes, ending up in tiny air sacs called "alveoli." You have about 300 million alveoli. The oxygen in the air seeps through the alveoli into tiny, thin-walled blood vessels called "capillaries," and into the blood. The oxygen-rich blood is then pumped by the heart to all your body's tissues. The blood also collects waste products from the tissues, including carbon dioxide, and brings them back to the lungs so they can be breathed out. Any irritants, such as dust particles are expelled when you sneeze. The air rushes out of your nasal passages at 100 mph.

HOLDING YOUR BREATH UNDERWATER

You can probably hold your breath underwater for about a minute. See how that compares to these creatures:

Sperm whale...112 mins
Seal...22 mins
Hippopotamus...15 mins
Platypus...10 mins
Sea otter...5 mins
Human pearl diver..2.5 mins
Polar bear...1.5 mins

FREE-DIVING FEATS

CONSTANT BALLAST
The diver swims as deep as he or she can without the assistance of extra weight. The world record is held by Carlos Coste of Venezuela, who dived 344 feet (105 m) underwater.

STATIC APNOEA
The diver holds his or her breath for as long as possible while floating face-down in a swimming pool. The world

record is held by Tom Sietas of Germany, who stayed
underwater for 9 minutes, 8 seconds.

DYNAMIC APNOEA

The diver swims as far as possible underwater.
The world record is held by Stig Aavall Severinsen
of Denmark, who swam nearly 740 feet (225 m)
without taking a breath.

When you are resting you breathe about 12-15 times
every minute. If you are exercising, you may breathe
more than 60 times a minute in order to get more
oxygen into your body.

DEEP-SEA DIVING SICKNESS

If a deep-sea diver surfaces too rapidly, nitrogen bubbles
form in the body causing painful joints, vertigo (dizziness
and loss of balance), nausea, and, in severe cases,
death. Some of the first humans to experience deep-sea
diving sickness, also known as the "Bends," were the
pearl divers of Polynesia. For hundreds of years,
the pearl divers have been swimming down to depths
of 130 feet (40 m) many times a day without a breathing
apparatus. Years before it was fully understood, the
pearl divers were reporting the symptoms of diving
sickness. Their name for it is *taravana*, which means
"to fall crazily."

Even sperm whales are not immune to deep-sea diving
sickness. These whales are known to spend
up to a two hours thousands of feet underwater,
before surfacing to breathe. They avoid injury by
ascending slowly but, just like divers, accidents
and disturbances sometimes force them up to
the surface at dangerous speeds.

HORMONES

Hormones are chemicals produced by the body's "endocrine" glands. They are released into the bloodstream and travel around the body where they affect certain areas. They are used to control and maintain bodily processes, such as growth. Some key hormones include:

INSULIN is produced by the pancreas. It controls the body's blood sugar level.

ADRENALINE is produced in the adrenal glands on the kidneys. It prepares the body to cope with moments of stress, overwork, or danger.

ESTROGEN is the sex hormone produced in a woman's ovaries. It affects the development and control of sexual characteristics such as the female body shape, breasts, and egg release.

TESTOSTERONE is the sex hormone produced in a man's testes. It affects the development and control of sexual characteristics such as the male body shape, hair growth, and sperm production.

STARING COMPETITION

In this game, two people lock eyes with each other and both try not to be the first to blink, flinch, or look away. The first to break the stare loses. Staring competitions can also be played with household pets. Cats are particularly tough opponents. Goldfish are unbeatable because they don't have eyelids.

HEARING

Sounds are made when something moves or vibrates. Sound vibrations travel through the air at a speed of 1,125 feet (343 m) per second. By trapping these sounds, your ears relay information to your brain about the type of sound and where it is coming from.

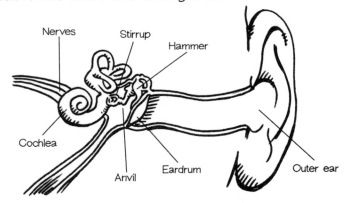

OUTER EAR: The outer ear funnels sound waves down a narrow tunnel that leads about 3/4-1 inch (2-3 cm) into your head.

EARDRUM: Stretched across the end of the tunnel is a membrane called the eardrum. The sound vibrations hit the drum, which shakes. On the other side of the membrane are three tiny bones called the hammer, anvil, and stirrup.

COCHLEA: The tiny bones carry the vibrations across an air-filled gap to the "cochlea," which resembles a snail's shell filled with fluid. The vibrations ripple over thousands of microscopic hairs, which produce nerve signals.

BRAIN: The nerve signals are sent to the brain. Every type of sound makes the hairs produce different nerve signals, which are interpreted by the brain as sounds.

ACTUAL BODY LANGUAGE

FARTS

The sound of a fart is the vibration of your anus that occurs when gas escapes— just like when you make farty sounds with your mouth.

BURPS

When you burp, air rushes back up from your insides and pushes open a special hatch at the back of your mouth called the "epiglottis." The epiglottis usually stops food from going down the wrong way when you swallow. "Burp!" is the sound it makes when it flaps back.

KNUCKLE CRACKS

When you link the fingers of both hands and stretch them by pushing them away from you, you might hear a *"crack!"* from one or more knuckles. What you are actually doing is pulling the bones of your knuckle joint apart ever so slightly. Like any good stretch, it can be a nice feeling as the pressure is taken off your bones. The cracking sound is bubbles of air quickly forming in the fluid between the joints.

EAR POPS

This is the sound of a small bubble of air entering your ear from the back of your nose. It happens when the air pressure changes as you go up or down suddenly in a lift or an airplane. Your eardrum needs a pocket of air on both sides to pick up sound vibrations so that you can hear properly. When the air pressure is not equal on both sides, your ear feels blocked. If you swallow, or pinch your nose and blow, the pressure equalizes with a *"pop!"* and you can hear again.

THE GORY RAINBOW

PURPLE BRUISE
When you get a heavy knock, thousands of tiny blood vessels are broken in your skin and a big purple bruise appears. In a day or two, it turns blue or black. Next, it goes greenish-yellow. In a couple of weeks, it turns light brown as your body breaks down the leaked blood cells and absorbs them back into your system. Then it disappears.

BLUE SKIN
When you are really cold, your body diverts blood from your skin to your vital organs, so that the most important parts of your body can stay warm and keep working. The reduced circulation leads to a lack of oxygen in the blood near the skin. Oxygen-poor blood is blue, and so your skin takes on a bluish tinge.

BROWN POO
The brown color of poo is caused by bile, a digestive juice secreted by your liver, which is then decomposed by bacteria in your intestines.

RED BLOOD
Blood is red because it contains iron-rich proteins called "hemoglobin" that pick up oxygen from the lungs and carry it around the body. Oxygen-rich blood is bright red.

YELLOW EARWAX
Fresh earwax is yellow, while older earwax is brown or even black. It can be either dry or sticky. It oozes from glands in your inner ear to trap dirt and any creepy-crawlies that sneak inside.

TYPES OF FOSSILS

Fossils are the physical evidence left by creatures that lived long ago. When plants and animals die, their bodies usually rot away. Sometimes, however, their bodies are covered with sediment, which builds up year after year. Over millions of years the sediment turns to rock, and in that rock fossils form. Here are some of the different types of fossil:

BODY FOSSILS
These form when chemicals in the rock seep into the teeth and bones of the animal's skeleton, causing them to harden.

MOLD FOSSILS
Mold fossils are body-shaped spaces found in rock. They form when a body gets covered in sediment then rots away, leaving a hole.

CAST FOSSILS
These form when rock minerals fill the body-shaped holes described above.

MUMMIFIED FOSSILS
Very occasionally animals such as dinosaurs are found with their skin and muscles preserved. These fossils form when the body of the animal dries out in a process called "mummification," before the flesh can rot.

TRACE FOSSILS
These are signs of the existence of dinosaurs that have become fossilized, such as footprints, dung, or half-eaten plants.

SCIENTIFIC CLASSIFICATION OF HUMANS

All living things can be classified into groups that share characteristics. The groups progress from the general (we are animals) to the more specific (we are primates) to the precise (we are homo sapiens).

Kingdom: Animalia

Phylum: Chordata

Class: Mammalia

Order: Primates

Family: Hominidae

Genus: Homo

Species: Sapiens

OLD SPICE

Your senses of taste and smell decrease as you get older. This is why older people tend to like foods that young people find too strong.

EATING A BALANCED DIET

Nutritionists recommend that we eat the following amounts of each sort of food every day.

Bread/Cereal
(six or
more servings)

Milk/Cheese/Yogurt
(two servings)

Vegetables
(three to
five servings)

Fruit (two to
four servings)

Meat/Fish/Soy
(two servings)

Fats/Oils/
Sweets
(not often)

THE MAJOR FOOD GROUPS AND WHAT YOU NEED THEM FOR

Carbohydrates..Energy
(cereal, bread, potatoes, pasta)

Proteins...................................Growing, body-building, and repair
(fish, meat, milk, cheese, soy)

Fats and oils..............................Energy, body-repair, hormones
(cooking oil, butter, nuts, and seeds)

Fiber..Digestion
(wholegrain cereals, fruit, and vegetables)

Vitamins and minerals............................All-around good health
(fruit, vegetables, dairy products, fish, cereals, liver)

CALORIES

The energy content of food is measured in "kilo calories" (kcal). One kilo calorie is the energy required to heat 1 kg of water by 1°C. You need calories from your food in order to grow, exercise, and perform functions such as breathing, keeping warm, and pumping your blood. If you eat fewer calories than your body needs you will lose weight. If you eat more calories than your body needs you will gain weight. To lose 1 lb. (0.45 kg) you would have to eat 3,500 kilo calories fewer than you use, and to gain 1 lb. (0.45 kg) you would have to eat 3,500 kilo calories more than you use. The number of calories you need per day varies from person to person, and depends on age and sex. Here is a rough guide:

KILO CALORIES REQUIRED PER DAY

AGE	BOYS	GIRLS
1-4 years	1,200	1,100
5-10 years	1,800	1,600
11-14 years	2,200	1,800
15-18 years	2,800	2,100
Adult	2,500	2,000

> You consume one tenth of a calorie
> every time you lick a stamp.

YOU ARE BIPEDAL

Walking upright on two legs is known as "bipedalism." It's the single most important difference between humans and apes.

It is thought that bipedalism evolved as a strategy for living on the ground when climate change destroyed the forests, leaving wide open spaces with no trees.

BODY PARTS NAMED AFTER PEOPLE

ACHILLES TENDON
Achilles, Greek mythological character
Attaches your calf muscles to your heel bone.

ADAM'S APPLE
Adam, Biblical character
Part of the voice box.

COOPER'S LIGAMENTS
Sir Astley Paston Cooper, English surgeon and anatomist
Cooper's ligaments are the connective tissues in the
breast. They weaken with age, causing the breasts to
droop (Cooper's Droop).

DARWIN'S TUBERCLE
Charles Darwin, British naturalist
The point of the ear. It thickens into "cauliflower ears"
when damaged—often seen on boxers.

FALLOPIAN TUBES
Gabrielle Falloppio, sixteenth-century anatomist
A pair of tubes, one leading from each of a woman's
ovaries to her womb.

THE BODY FARM

The body farm is a three-acre plot of land in Tennessee.
Otherwise known as the University of Tennessee Forensic
Anthropology Facility, it is used to study the decomposition
of human bodies. Dead bodies are placed in various
situations around the farm, such as in cars, in the open air
or in shallow graves, and their decomposition is closely
monitored. The information helps police and forensic
scientists determine how long a body has been dead, and
so helps to solve crimes. So far, more than 300 people
have donated their bodies to the farm.

ARE YOU IN CLASSICAL PROPORTION?

YOUR HEIGHT IS EQUAL TO...
...ten times the length of your hand.

...five times the distance from your elbow to the tip of your hand.

...four times the width of your shoulders.

...the distance from the fingertips of one outstretched hand to the other.

THE LENGTH OF YOUR FACE IS EQUAL TO...
...three times the distance from the bottom of your chin to your nostrils.

...three times the distance from your hairline to your eyebrows.

...three times the length of your ear.

Coronary heart disease is the most common cause of sudden death, and accounts for 12% of all deaths worldwide. The main factors that put an individual at risk of the disease are cigarette smoking, high blood pressure, and high levels of cholesterol.

INFECTION

If your outer defense system—the skin—is breached with a cut or wound, germs try to creep inside. Luckily, your body has back-up defenses that swing into action.

INFLAMMATION

Your skin's damaged tissues release chemicals that widen the blood vessels and make them leak. The area becomes red, warm, and swollen as extra blood arrives on the scene, and the repairing fluids seep out and into the damaged tissues.

FEVER

If need be, the body raises its temperature above its normal 98.6°F (37°C) as germs often cannot survive above this temperature. This makes you sweat and shiver.

THE ATTACK TROOPS

White blood cells rush to the scene. Their mission is to surround and destroy the invader. Also present in white blood cells are chemicals called "antibodies" that are programmed to remember the invaders, so that next time they can be destroyed without hesitation. This gives a person long-term protection against a particular germ, known as "immunity."

MIKE THE HEADLESS CHICKEN

Mike the Headless Chicken lived for 18 months without a head. A farmer had lopped it off with an axe on September 10, 1945, but not having a head didn't bother Mike at all. The farmer dripped food down the chicken's throat with a pipette. Mike even tried to preen himself with his nonexistent head. Scientists had an explanation: they said that the brain stem, where most of a chicken's reflex actions are located, was largely unharmed.

ANCIENT HERBAL POISONS

ACONITE

The leaves of the aconite flower were picked in June and pulped into a poisonous juice. It was also known as "wolfsbane," because arrows tipped with aconite were used to kill wolves.

DEADLY NIGHTSHADE

Women used to drop the juice of the deadly nightshade flower into their eyes to dilate their pupils. It became known as belladonna, which is Italian for "beautiful woman." Symptoms of belladonna poisoning include extreme dryness of the mouth and throat, and convulsions.

HEMLOCK

In Ancient Greece, hemlock was called "conium," which means "to whirl about." This was because one of the symptoms of hemlock poisoning is vertigo. Another is numbness, which spreads inward until the heart and lungs are paralyzed. People have been known to mistake hemlock roots for parsnips and the leaves for parsley, and accidentally poison themselves.

MUSHROOMS

Some mushrooms are poisonous and can cause headaches, delirium, and fever. In extreme cases the heart can stop and the person can die.

EYE-POPPING QUEEN

The world record for eyeball popping is held by Kim Goodman of the United States. She can pop her eyeballs out almost one-half inch (11 mm) from their sockets.

THE BODY-PART OLYMPICS

THE FACIAL DECATHLON

1. Roll your tongue.

2. Wiggle your ears.

3. Raise one eyebrow.

4. Turn your eyelids inside out.

5. Cross your eyes.

6. Move your eyes independently of one another.

7. Touch your nose with your tongue.

8. Flare your nostrils ten times without moving your eyebrows.

9. Stretch your mouth into a diagonal line.

10. Move your hair without touching it.

THE HAND PENTATHLON

1. Bend the tips of your fingers while keeping the rest of your fingers straight.

2. Bend your thumb back to touch your wrist.

3. Do the Vulcan salute. Hold your palm outwards then place your fingers in a V shape by separating your ring and middle fingers, keeping your others together.

4. Press both hands together and bend your knuckles to make a farty noise.

5. Hold both hands in front of you. Touch the tips of your middle fingers together and do the Mexican Wave.

COMMON SPORTING INJURIES

SPRAINED ANKLE: If your ankle bends the wrong way, the muscles and ligaments in the joint stretch. The ankle swells and stiffens, and needs rest and support for a few days.

STITCH: The lining of the abdomen, called the "parietal peritoneum," is sensitive to movement. When you exercise, your intestines jiggle around and disturb this lining, and the friction causes a sharp stabbing pain.

CRAMP: Occurs when the blood flow is not fast enough to take away the waste products of exercise, or if the muscle is squashed or used in repetitive movements. The muscle goes into a spasm, and becomes hard and tense.

DISLOCATED JOINT: A joint dislocates when the ends of its bones slip from their usual positions. The dislocation stretches or tears the ligaments holding the bones in position, and damages blood vessels, nerves, and other parts, causing pain and swelling.

GENES

In sexual reproduction, the way the offspring's body is put together is determined by tiny parcels of information called "genes." Genes are strands of a molecule called DNA, short for "deoxyribonucleic acid," which contains the instructions for how to build an organism. Your genes might contain instructions for a big nose, small ears, green eyes, or long legs. You get some genes from your dad, some from your mom, some from your grandparents, and some from ancestors you've never even met.

If your father has a big nose and your mother has a little nose, this doesn't mean you'll get a medium-sized nose. The two parcels of information about the size of a nose will have been delivered to you, but only one is opened. The unopened one remains in a gene backroom. It may be opened again in your children, or your children's children, and so on.

CLONES

Reproductive cloning can be used to make an exact genetic copy of an existing animal. To do this, scientists remove the genetic information from a reproductive egg and replace it with genetic information from the animal they want to clone. An electric current or chemicals are then applied to make the egg develop. When it has grown big enough, the developed egg is transferred to the womb of a female animal, where it continues to develop until birth.

Successfully cloned animals include:
Dolly the sheep • Idaho Gem the mule • CC the kitten •
Five piglets called Noel, Angel, Star, Joy, and Mary.

FORENSIC SCIENCE

Forensic science studies human corpses to discover the time and cause of death. In criminal investigations, forensic scientists often have to inspect the whole crime scene. There are three main branches of forensic science.

1. Forensic pathology examines the body to look for the cause of death, such as wounds or traces of poison.

2. Forensic entomology studies the insects found in corpses for clues that might shed light on the time of death, such as the development of maggots.

3. Forensic anthropology studies skeletons and human remains for clues as to the identity, race, and sex of the dead person.

Every single cell in your body contains unique DNA. DNA found at crime scenes can help forensic detectives solve crimes. The tiniest hair, piece of skin, drop of blood, or any other body part can be enough to identify the criminal.

You share 99.9% of your DNA with every other person on Earth. This means that a minuscule amount of DNA accounts for all the differences in the human race.